Defining Success *On Your Own Terms*

MAKING FLEX WORK

Wendy A. Cocke

Publishing support provided by
Ignite Press
5070 N. Sixth St. #189
Fresno, CA 93710
www.IgnitePress.us

ISBN: 979-8-9863049-0-8
ISBN: 979-8-9863049-1-5 (Ebook)

For bulk purchase and for booking, contact:

Wendy Cocke
wendy.anderson.cocke@gmail.com
www.makingflexwork.com

Library of Congress Control Number: 2022909485

Cover design by Annatto LLC
Edited by Elizabeth Arterberry
Interior design by Jetlaunch Layout Services

FIRST EDITION

*I dedicate this book to my dad, who never got the chance to read it,
but would have single-handedly purchased enough copies
to put it on the New York Times bestseller list
if he'd had the opportunity.*

Acknowledgments

To My Family: Andy, AJ, Lily, Mom, and Mamaw

Thank you for putting up with me using voice-to-text for hours in the car, giving me grace as I charted a path that was unfamiliar to all of us, and pretending to be excited about each and every tiny milestone along the way. You are my biggest cheerleaders.

To My Inspiration: Angela Mitchell, Bill Swanger, Brian Nelson, Christi Fiorentini, John Rotella, Kate Dziak, Sarah Wells, and all the others named and unnamed

Thank you for being willing to be a part of my story. The immediate "yes" from each of you when I asked if I could include you, the full creative freedom you gave me to tell your stories, and your willingness to fill in the blanks when

I couldn't remember all the details can't be replaced. You are literally the secret sauce to this book. Without your contributions in my career, I wouldn't have the perspective, experiences, or position to write a book at all!

To My Creative Support: Lindsay Boseman (Annatto LLC) and Lesly Gregory

Thank you for selflessly providing your skills to fill in my gaps. Lesly, your pre-read gave me confidence to move forward, and the countless hours of editing not only made the document flow, but removed my habitual double space after a period (when did that change?). Lindsay, you provided the excitement and talent to transform my brand and artwork from a bunch of words into something beautiful. Without you, I wouldn't have this amazing cover, my Engineering Leadership Solutions logo, or anything on my website.

To My Emotional Support: Jennifer Barrett, Jordan Snow, Kay Starnes, and Sarah Wells

Thank you for continually telling me how great this book was going to be when my imposter syndrome kicked in. Also, thank you for test-driving the content, the tools, and the format when the book was little more than some random stories in a Google doc. There were lots of days when I would remind myself that I am an engineer, not a writer, and one of you would be there to make sure I didn't walk away.

To My Editorial Board: Andy Cocke, Cathy Fyock, Casey Dusenbery, Emily Smith, Jesscia van Derven, Randy Watson, and Rhonda Gibby

Thank you for making the time to not only read the book, but also for providing such amazing feedback in terms of content, word choice, and organization. You represent a cross-section of my life, and this book would look so different without your fingerprints. Besides, if a reader doesn't like something, I can likely find at least one of you who can share the blame with me.

Table of Contents

Introduction

Let's talk about balance. Is there even such a thing? I believe the answer to this question is yes: all aspects of your life can be in balance as long as you define the right time horizon.

As a wife and mother of two children with a professional job—who also has some responsibility for my mother and grandmother (who live next-door to us)—I am on a never-ending search for balance. For more than a decade, I have read through the "who's who" of work-life balance books, talked to friends over coffee or drinks, engaged with my peers on social media, and tried more techniques than I want to admit. My guess is that if you picked up this book, then at least a part of my list (and maybe more) seems very familiar to you.

You are not alone. I can tell you that, on any given day, my life is most definitely out of balance. Some days I am an excellent wife, other days I excel at motherhood, and some days I am a model employee, but there are rarely days when I am amazing at all three at once. On the average, though, I think my co-workers and my family would give me a solid A. Thankfully, I'm not graded on a daily basis, and neither are you.

You may spend time each day reflecting on how you measured up to your own expectations, but most people think of you as an aggregate of their experiences with you. If you can shift how you evaluate yourself to be more in line with how you evaluate others (meaning that you make your time horizon long enough to account for the ups and downs), then you can achieve balance.

Depending on where you are in your career, your caregiving, and your self-care, one aspect of your life may need to take precedence over the others. That's okay. As long as you don't totally neglect any single part of your life, it is possible to maintain a macro-level of balance.

What Success Means to Me

I started my career like a lot of people: working for a Fortune 100 company right out of college. I'm a chemical engineer, so I was over the moon when I landed my ideal job in Research and Development. I spent ten years moving up that ladder. I did the rounds through all of the departments and all different types of project work.

Outside of work, I was involved in professional societies, had fun with my friends, met my husband, fell in love, and got married. I felt successful. It wasn't until I was pregnant with our first child that I even stopped to think about what I actually wanted. Until that point, I had just been following the predetermined path.

Before my son was born, my husband and I had a lot of conversations about balancing parenting and our careers (including the potential that I would quit my job to be a full-time stay-at-home mom). In the end, we decided to try just "doing it all." I hadn't been back to work for three months before I realized that this strategy wasn't going to work for me. That's when I started to investigate flexible work arrangements, only to find that, for me, in my role, the options were (or at least seemed to be) very limited. My leaders and mentors sadly shared with me that if I negotiated anything other than a traditional schedule, then my career would be negatively impacted. One even went so far as to warn me that I might never be promoted again!

It took me eleven months to get that first flexible work arrangement, but since that time, I have led global project teams, transitioned from being an individual contributor to a director in large corporations (before eventually opening my own management consulting company, Engineering Leadership Solutions), and continued to grow my family, all while still being involved in all the activities that are important to me. That's what success looks like to me!

Your definition of success is likely different, and that's okay. As a matter of fact, it is more than okay; it's perfect. The fact that we each get to define success on our terms is what makes this process so great. Whatever it is you want, I hope that I can be a part of that process. Together, I know that we can get what you need and want to be successful as well.

How Do You Get There?

"Ask for what you want." That's the general advice the world gives people (specifically women) when it comes to succeeding in the corporate world, but that's only half the advice you actually need. In my experience, this half-story is the reason that most people fail at getting what they want.

Asking for what you want is the first half, but the other half is phrasing your needs in a way that gives your company what they need. It's not as tricky as it sounds, as long as you are willing to put on your business hat while you are thinking about yourself.

As an employee, you can improve your odds of success by bringing the business case with you to the first (and every subsequent) discussion. To target your thinking, you can ask yourself these questions so that you are prepared to articulate not only what you want, but how it can be accomplished within your organization:

- Will it allow you to work more focused hours?
- Will it cut down on the cost of business travel?
- Will it open you up for communication with colleagues or teammates in other regions of the world more easily?

How do I know it can be done? I know because I've worked a flexible schedule for over a decade and have not seen it slow down my career ambitions or my impact on the business. In fact, I've gotten more opportunities and faster promotions since securing my flexible work arrangement.

During this time, I have had many people ask me how I did it and how they can make one that works for them. I always give the same two pieces of advice, so here they are for you. We will dig more into this advice throughout the book, but even if you stop reading here, I want to make sure you hear this:

Think about the gap between what you are doing today and what you want to be doing in the future. There may be ways to close it without having to go through a formal flexible work arrangement process.

Maybe you are like I was, giving your job every free moment instead of paying attention to when you are working. To top it off, I wasn't focused on the task at hand while I was working because I felt like I needed to make everything fit, and that was actually reducing my productivity.

By being intentional in how you spend your time, you may find that you can get what you want without having to ask anyone for anything.

The EVALuation method outlined in this book (and on my website www.makingflexwork.com) will help you to be intentional and to find time in your schedule that you didn't know you had.

Make sure that you build enough flexibility on the personal side of the equation so your employer never feels pain as a result of the accommodations they give you. If they can't get the work done with you, they will get it done without you.

As a manager (even one who supports all types of flexibility), it is not always easy to see how a request for a flexible work arrangement from your employee is anything but a loss for the business. What usually happens is that someone comes to you asking for accommodations, but they haven't thought through the potential ways they can ensure the job will continue to get done.

I challenge you to present how you plan to be flexible in your personal life as well. How much notice do you need to change your plans? How will you support an emergency in the business? What will you do to ensure the company always wins?

Doing that won't guarantee that you get your "yes," but it will make giving you a "no" even harder, and it highlights that you are strongly committed to the success of the broader organization (something that I have personally leveraged to move up the management ladder while working a flexible schedule).

As you read this book, I encourage you to think about the grace you give others, and about how you can apply that benefit of the doubt to yourself as well. Give yourself some grace—you don't have to be all things, to all people, all the time.

1

Why Are You Here?

FLEXIBLE WORK, HYBRID work, non-traditional work: it doesn't matter what you call it, it is about balancing your life in such a way that work fits best for you. Take a moment to reflect on how you feel about each of the arrangements listed below.

Traditional 9-5
Hybrid Location
Split Schedule
Fully Remote
Part-Time

Do you recognize them? Do any of them scare you? Do any of them excite you? No matter how you feel, or what you do or do not know about them, it is okay. This is a journey and we will get through it together.

Everyone has a unique story, a specific reason to want more flexibility, but we *all* want to feel successful. Luckily, there isn't a single definition of success, so you are allowed to define it for yourself. That's the great thing about it: it is up to each of us to define. The power is yours.

- Do you feel like you can't balance all of the pieces of your life?
- Do you wish you had more time with your family?
- Do you think you work too much?
- Do you believe that you could end each day feeling happier if you just made a few changes to your schedule?
- Do you have people working for you asking for more flexibility in their job?
- Do you dread the idea of working full-time in a traditional office setting?

These are just a few of the reasons people have come to me to explore the idea of nontraditional work schedules over the years, and, today more than ever, people are rethinking the way they do traditional work.

If you have picked up this book, it is likely you answered yes to one or more of the questions above. If so, I know this book can help you find what you are looking for.

I am confident in making this assertion because I have successfully maintained a flexible work arrangement while working for large corporations for over half of my professional career. During that time, I led medical device product launches, global teams, and cross-functional project portfolios. I did it, and I know you can, too.

As you read through this book, you may be challenged to think about your work differently and even rethink the ideal work arrangement you currently have in your head. I encourage you to embrace new ideas and look for ways to incorporate them into your framework. The most important thing to keep in mind is that there is no right or wrong way to achieve success; it is a journey. What works for you today may not work for you tomorrow, but be willing to give yourself grace and take it one day at a time.

If It Wasn't Flexible, It Would Just Be Called the "Work Arrangement"

It's called a "flexible work arrangement" because it's flexible. If it wasn't flexible, it would just be called the "work arrangement." I can't count the number of times I have told someone this. Most people smile and nod when I say it, but a person's lack of understanding of the term is the biggest obstacle to maintaining a flexible work arrangement. Over the last decade, when I have asked people about what they want out of a flexible work arrangement, they give me a lot of requirements, but most of them bring up something that is not particularly flexible. This may be child care, parent care, or a side hustle. The point is that they simply want to work reduced hours, or that they would prefer to have a non-traditional schedule... not a flexible schedule.

They may want to come in late, leave early, not work this day or that day, but they still want a predictable schedule. That is not a flexible work arrangement. A flexible work arrangement is one in which you can deliver what the company needs without a standard work schedule. This may mean that you spend part of your time working at home and part in the office, some time on the road and some at your normal location, or work fewer hours altogether. It simply means you want more flexibility.

The other misconception is that flexibility is required from both the employee and the company. While employers may flex some traditional terms, the need for the employee to deliver results will not change. The burden of flexibility belongs to the employee. (Yes, I know this isn't a popular opinion).

In order to be successful, I suggest that you set up your life in such a way that you can be flexible. Just saying no to a project or task because it is not in your predefined schedule is not a way to be successful in a flexible work arrangement. If your children go to a childcare facility on the days you are scheduled to work, but not on the days you aren't, you should have a plan in place in the event that you need to work on a non-scheduled day. If you have coverage at home for the hours you are away, you also need to have the option for coverage on the hours you would normally be at home, just in case you are needed longer.

You must understand that the company is responsible for getting the same amount of work done regardless of your own desires and obligations. It is up to you to explain to the company how they will not lose out in this arrangement. If they are going to lose by keeping you on board, they'll find someone else and win without you.

The Company Will Always Ask for More

Corporations are designed to take everything you give them and then ask for more. There is never such a thing as "enough." Therefore, it is up to you to set boundaries and to stick to them.

> It is up to you to set boundaries and to stick to them.

Since the time of the industrial revolution, corporations have depended on finding ways to get more out of their human capital to be successful.

"Do more with less."

"Be more efficient."

"Look for opportunities to be more lean."

"Implement continuous improvement efforts."

These are all concepts centered on a business' need to get as much as possible from their employees. At a very fundamental level, this is because once an employee is hired, they become a fixed cost against the company's bottom line, so the only way to improve their return on investment in human capital is to get more out of that employee.

This isn't to say that businesses are bad; they just have a different goal than a person (or even the people who lead them). Results are critical for a successful business, and the most successful ones have leaders who know that supporting their employees is the number one way to drive business results. If you always keep this in mind, you will be better positioned to negotiate and maintain your boundaries.

It is not about how many hours you work, but what you deliver for the company that ultimately matters. Understanding what is important to the business and excelling in those areas is more critical than just showing up. If you do this correctly, most people won't even know you are doing it unless you tell them. This doesn't mean that you have to hide it, but it should never be an issue for your coworkers.

So, how do you establish healthy work-life boundaries, especially if you haven't done so before? It is possible you may not have set appropriate boundaries at work yet, so adjusting from your current reality to your ideal state may take several steps.

Start by identifying your ideal work arrangement and see how far away it is from your current reality. Migrating to this ideal state will not happen overnight, but having a goal gives you something specific to work toward.

Before we move on, here are some questions to consider:

- What does your current work schedule look like?
- What are you trying to achieve?
- What would your ideal daily/weekly schedule look like?

- What would be different in your life if you had your ideal schedule?
- What are you willing to do to make your ideal schedule a reality?

After you've established where you want to end up, you'll need to figure out how to get there. It will take thought, planning, patience, and self-advocacy. I know you can do it, but, before we get there, I'll share my story and the steps I took to get the flexible work arrangement that worked for me.

2

My Journey from Overwhelmed Employee to Successfully Flexible Leader

WHILE I SPENT most of my corporate life working a flexible arrangement (in my case, 32 hours per week—aka part-time), getting there meant I had to convince my leader to make the most important decision of my career. Yes, you read that correctly, *he* had to make the most important decision of my career. Getting a "yes" was critically important to me and my family, but to him, it was just another decision—specifically, one that was going to cause him heartburn. As a matter of fact, getting him to make that decision took me almost eleven months!

Phase 1: The Proposal

The year was 2010. I was thirty years old, a new mother, and an engineer who was successfully leading a variety of engineering projects at a Fortune 100 company—and I was drowning. I was frustrated with my husband, my child, my coworkers, and, let's be honest, I was just tired. I couldn't find any relief and my guilt was through the roof. I wanted to be a perfect mother, a perfect wife, and a perfect employee, but, although everyone else would have given me at least a B+, I felt like I was failing at everything. This isn't uncommon among working mothers (especially the highly-driven Type A ones), and, for me, it was torture. I am lucky enough to have a successful husband, which gave me some options that not everyone has. That being said, I encourage you to use what you have; that's why you have it.

> Use what you have; that's why you have it.

I was working for a team leader who happened to be a good friend and just a few years ahead of me professionally, so I told him that I needed to drop my hours. He was still green in his first people-leader role, but he knew that I wasn't one to give up easily. He understood that if I was coming to him, then it must be a big deal. Although we quickly aligned on the idea of trying to find a way to let me work in a flexible work arrangement, neither of us actually knew how to do it.

Across the entire five-building work campus, there were only a handful of people who had non-traditional work arrangements, and only one was in a technical role. I reached out to her, got all the information she had, and got to work. In my case, the first step was the completion of a "Flexible Work Arrangement Form," which required signatures from my team leader, my department vice president, and my human resources representative. Getting approval from my team leader was going to be easy, but I knew the other two would be a challenge. By the end of the month, my manager and I had agreed on an arrangement and we were ready to set up a discussion with our vice president.

Phase 2: The Roadblock

Then came the day that I still refer to as "the darkest day in my career."

That was the day I was called into another team leader's office and was presented with an "opportunity" to take over a very important project that had just failed its qualification. When

I say it failed, I don't mean, "Let's just write a rationale and retest it." I mean, "Wow, the product did *what?*"

They had already boxed up the equipment used for this project and shipped it to a new manufacturing facility. The team was going to have to regroup and look at both their expectations and the design—and maybe even the equipment. They had failed with flying colors, and I was being asked to step in as the new project manager to get it back on track and eventually to the market. This was exactly the type of project that would get me promoted and well-positioned for the next phase of my career. It was the kind of opportunity that, had it been presented to me three years prior, would have had my husband and me cracking open the champagne.

I should have been excited, but all I could think was that this was really going to put a wrench in my ability to go part-time. I tried to keep calm and asked for a little time to think about it. But, as with most corporate opportunities, it wasn't really much of a question and I knew that. I knew that I was supposed to act excited as I told them I was happy to accept the challenge of the new opportunity. Besides, these big projects don't just come around every day, and they certainly don't just pop up in a condition that allows the incoming leader to be the hero.

After lunch, I walked into the new team leader's office to turn him down.

"Thanks, but no thanks," I said to him. "I appreciate being considered, but I don't think this is the right role for me at this time. I will just keep my current job. I'm sure you can find someone else."

He changed his tactic and pitched his idea again. "If you take on this opportunity, you will be set up for the manager role you really want when the next one comes available."

"I get that this project will be good for my career, but I don't think it will be good for my family. Unfortunately, I have to pass."

He pitched it again, and I turned him down again. That's when it became clear that I didn't have a choice.

He said, "This project is really important to the company. If you aren't willing to do what it takes to get us where we need to go, then how can we trust you to manage a team in the future? Leaders need to put the company first. Managers understand that, by walking away, you will show that you are not cut out to be a manager."

As tears began to roll down my face, I asked how this would impact my ability to go part-time. The simple answer was that part-time would officially be off the table for me as a project leader. I got up without saying a word and walked out.

I walked out into a hallway lined with cubicles, my face still red and wet with tears, and immediately started looking for a place to breathe. Being a new mother, I knew there was a phone in the Mother's Room, so I quickly headed there. Upon arrival, I discovered it was locked and, behind the door, I could hear the sound of a pump. I didn't know where else to go, so I knocked and quietly shouted, "I need to come in, it's an emergency."

Like any new mother, my friend on the other side of the door didn't hesitate and quickly opened the door. I told her that I didn't want to bother her, just to use the phone. She understood and moved to the other side of the room.

I called my husband and gave him the full rundown, quickly moving from crying to anger. It was at that moment that I heard all I needed to hear. "Tell them you aren't taking their role and you quit... I'll go by later and get your stuff... Call me from the car... I love you."

I'm sure there were other words, but those were the only ones that mattered. I hung up the phone and took a deep breath.

My friend, however, had a different plan. Before I could thank her and walk out, she said words I will never forget. "If you quit, they win. Make them fire you. Make them pay you to leave."

Her words stopped me in my tracks. I realized that she was right. If I stormed back into the office and simply quit, then they would have to find someone else to do the job (maybe even her). But, if I could play their game using my rules, it was possible that I could actually change the future for those who followed me.

I walked back to the new leader's office, accepted the role, and was immediately escorted to a conference room where my new team was waiting to welcome me. To this day, I have no idea how long they had been sitting there, but I know that I walked in with a tear-streaked face and kicked off my first team meeting.

Phase 3: The Comeback

While I didn't let go of the idea of going part-time, I knew immediately that I was going to have to take a different path to it than I had originally planned. During that summer, I worked fewer hours than usual, but I didn't tell anyone. I made sure to get my work done, but I cut out the "extras."

- Where I might have previously picked up the slack for another team member, I instead forced myself to hold them accountable for their work.

- In instances where I could have completed something by the next day if I just worked later, I would suggest that I would have it done by the end of the week to pressure test the true urgency of the request.

- I challenged my perfectionism to identify when work was sufficient instead of spending more time to make it perfect.

- I became intentional with my time in the office as opposed to just floating along through the workday.

In addition to making me feel better about my overall balance, this approach had the side-effect of establishing the right boundaries with the new team right from the start, which would be critical to my overall success in managing the flexible work arrangement later in my journey. You might not have this luxury, but if you do, never let an organizational change slip by without assessing how you can use it to your advantage.

By the end of summer, the project was on track and I had built some credibility with my new leadership. I used this as the chance to ask again about the potential for part-time work. This time, how-ever, I didn't talk to my team leader or his leader. Instead, I went directly to the vice president who would have to sign the

> Never let an organizational change slip by without assessing how you can use it to your advantage.

form. As a matter of fact, I asked him three times that fall. Each time, he found new ways to tell me no, and each time, I would retreat and regroup.

Just after New Year's, I made the decision to take a more rad-ical approach and pulled out my last card. I popped into the vice president's office for a chat on another topic, but before I left, I made sure to address my desire to go part-time.

"I am really struggling with being both a good mom and a good employee, and I don't know what to do. I don't want to have to walk away from the career I worked so hard to build, but I don't think I have any other options," I told him.

He just sat there quietly, stunned, as I continued, "I am so sad to have to choose, but my husband and I have talked it all through. I am going to need to step away from this project leader role. I would love to stay as a part of the team if you can move me to a different job that will allow me to work part-time, but if that isn't a possibility, I am going to have to leave the company. I have to do what is best for my family."

I didn't quit, but I got dangerously close. (I do not necessarily recommend this approach unless you really are ready to walk out, but I want to be candid with you about what I did in case you find yourself in the same position of desperation. At least you will know you aren't alone.)

It wasn't until I had finished that he told me that he didn't want any of that for me either and said "maybe" we could try part-time for 90 days to see if it would work. Just like "no" is short for "not yet" in my personal dictionary, I consider "maybe" to be a pending "yes," so I started my part-time trial that day.

I returned to my desk and told my team that I was going to test out a part-time schedule for the next three months, and that I needed their help. I told them that if anything didn't seem to be working, I needed to know right away, and I would make any adjustments—this was an experiment, and we were all a part of it. This is where the hard work of building a trusting team atmosphere paid off; they were all immediately supportive.

Over the next few months, I listened to feedback, tried different things, and kept the lines of communication open with the team. What I didn't do was keep reminding the leaders that I wasn't working full time. I just did my work. As the 90 days wrapped up, I sent a quick email to everyone I worked with asking for feedback on my part-time trial. I compiled the results, copied all of my leaders, and set up a meeting to discuss next steps. I was feeling good until the vice president declined my meeting.

I got up and (as I sometimes do) let my emotions take over as I stormed down the long hallway toward his office. As I approached, he stepped out and headed my way. He told me that he was surprised by my meeting request because he didn't know I had started the 90-day trial, but he had skimmed the feedback and had no reason not to sign my form. I got the "yes!"

As with many things in your career, you might not get the "yes" when you want it or in the way you want it, but if it is important, don't take "no" at face value. Use it as fuel to do more homework, to try again, and to change your approach. If it is important to you, then you should fight for it.

Phase 4: The Move to Leadership

A few years later, there was an opening to lead a team I had been a part of earlier in my career where I loved the people and the work. This was my moment to make the leap into management. It was perfect, except for the fact that no one in the organization had ever been a people-leader while working with a part-time arrangement. To add to the complication, this time I was pregnant with my second child. But I'm no quitter, so it was game on.

I applied with confidence and quickly started assessing the competition. I was clearly the right choice, and I knew it. I wasn't willing to compromise on the part-time arrangement, but I didn't tell anyone that (they didn't need to know). I went through the full recruiting process, the multiple rounds, the hours of interviews, and then I got the offer.

It was only at that moment I told him that I wasn't willing to give up my part-time status for the promotion. I also told him I was confident in my ability to do the job within my current hours. I even went a step further, telling him that I thought this managerial role would be easier because all my teammates would be in the same office, while the project team I was currently leading was scattered around the world (spanning four time zones and three countries).

He didn't buy it. He explained that the role was full-time and that now he would need to rethink his decision. I told him that I understood and walked away. Over the next six months, my belly got visibly larger. Each time we met, he would ask if I had thought any more about the role, and I would ask him if he had thought any more about letting me try it part-time. It appeared that we were in a stalemate, but that was fine with me since I had the leverage. I had a job I liked, but he didn't have a manager—remember, not every position of power in a negotiation is obvious.

The week before my due date, he made his decision and offered me the job while agreeing to maintain my part-time status. We finished the paperwork on Thursday afternoon, he made my announcement to the team on Friday, and I delivered my daughter the following Monday.

> Not every position of power in a negotiation is obvious.

Over the next ten years, I would move from manager to associate director, and eventually to director, without having to fight to stay part-time. Because I wasn't willing to give up at the first "no," I was committed to delivering excellent business results, and I found creative ways to make sure the company always came out ahead, I was able to use each new role to redefine success in my own terms and, in the process, I was able to help the leaders around me reimagine it too.

3

How to Get
Where You Want to Go:
The EVALuation Method

NOW THAT YOU have a better idea of what you want, there are a few easy steps that will help you get there. The first step is to understand your current spoken (and unspoken) work arrangement. The spoken agreement is usually the easy part. It includes the job you are being paid to do, the work product you are expected to deliver, and the work times and locations that are considered standard for your role or department. The unspoken part is slightly trickier. It consists of all the things you have been giving the company without even thinking about it: the hours you currently work, the times when it is okay to text or call you, the nights and weekends that you are willing to open your computer and work, etc. The list goes on and on.

Next, assess and optimize your current work arrangement as necessary within the constraints of those agreements. After that, you have to decide whether to use the optimized schedule or ask for changes beyond the scope of your current agreement. If you decide to ask for changes, you will need to be your own advocate while also practicing patience.

Finally, once you have an idea of what you are going to do, just try it. Don't worry if it doesn't go perfectly to plan during the first day, week, or even month. Learning to be flexible is the whole point of this journey anyway, so give yourself grace along the way.

Let's dig deeper into understanding and optimizing your current arrangement using the EVALuation method.

Every hour counts
Value optimized work
Assess the expectations
Leverage small changes

Step 1 – Every Hour Counts

Before you change anything, you must first know what you are currently doing. To do that, the first thing to do is to create an accurate log of what you are giving the company today. What are the hours that you are working? What are the hours you are not working? What are you doing during those working hours: is the work you're doing all focused on meeting the company's needs, or are you doing a mix of tasks for the company and yourself?

I suggest that you don't just think about it; instead, collect the actual data and get it on paper so you can see what needs to change. I have a trusted method that is completely customizable for everyone who uses it. The best part is that, once you have it, you can use it over and over again as your needs change. This will also provide you with a very clear picture of what you deliver for yourself and for the company right now.

On your paper, you may want to:

- Clock in and out as if you were punching a time clock to see how much you are actually working each day
- Record how often you switched between tasks (switching means stopping one thing to work on another before the first thing is complete)

- Record the number of times you started and stopped due to interruptions
- Record the time of the day you are the most productive
- Record when you feel the most in or off balance
- Record the days of the week you worked the most or least
- Record the amount of hours you are working

To learn more about journaling your time (including examples and tips), you can visit www.makingflexwork.com.

It is likely that journaling your time for as little as one to two weeks will provide you with some immediate changes you can make that will allow you to feel better about your balance. It is also likely that you will find waste in your day. As an engineer with a continuous improvement mindset, waste is one of those things that I look for around me. I focus on how I can streamline my work and be more efficient with my own time so that I can have all the things that I want.

My friend, Sarah, was struggling with her job. She called me crying about how she was failing… at everything. She was about to quit her job and called me, hoping I would be that supportive friend who would tell her that she was making the right choice for herself and her family. Unfortunately for her, that's not what she got from me. As I listened to her tell me about the hours she was working, the time she was missing with her boys, and the exhaustion that she was feeling, I knew exactly what she was going through.

Instead of supporting her instinct to run away, I challenged her to think differently about her time. I suggested she document what she was doing and even printed out a copy of my journal for her, drove to her house, and shoved it in her mailbox. The next morning I texted her a few words of encouragement and reminded her to start right away (even though it was a Friday).

When I checked back in with her the next week, she had already found more time. Here's what she realized:

- She spent far too much time cleaning up her inbox rather than focusing on the more significant work that needed to be accomplished. These were large blocks of time in which she was focused on responding to other people's needs instead of dedicating time to her own projects and deliverables.
- She'd go for extremely long periods of time without even taking a bathroom break. No wonder she wasn't feeling well! She realized she had blocked no time for herself throughout the day—which needed to change.
- She noticed how easily checking her inbox for a few minutes at night could easily turn into an hour of responding

to emails! These emails would still be there for her in the morning, and that hour was precious time she could be spending with her family.

Use this page to pause and reflect (maybe even journal). Here are a few questions to get you started:

- When do you typically start and stop working each day? Is it consistent or does it change throughout the week?

- How often do you switch tasks? Why? How does it feel? What would it feel like to complete one thing before moving on to something else?

- When do you feel the most in balance? How is that different from when you feel out of balance?

- How much are you actually working throughout the week? Is it more or less than you thought it was?

Step 2 – Value Optimized Work

Once you have your journal underway, the next step is to look for ways to optimize the way you work. Are you attempting to do things during the day that could easily be done before or after work, things that are taking work time away from the workday and therefore making you work longer because you are losing time? How many actual hours are you working? You have to be realistic with yourself if you want to succeed.

Yes, there are circumstances in which people need to work 60 to 70 hours a week continuously; there are industries where this is the norm. For most of us, however, we spend a significant chunk of time at work not doing work. How much time at work can you free up by eliminating those non-work tasks?

Are you stopping what you are doing and spending time walking back and forth between places that don't directly impact your ability to complete the task at hand?

- How many trips do you make to the printer?
- How many times do you refill your water or coffee?
- How many times do you have to walk back to get something you need but forgot to bring with you?

How many interruptions are you dealing with, and can any of them be prevented?

- Do you keep a candy dish on your desk to snack or for people to stop by to grab a piece, and then they end up lingering to chat?
- How often do you check your social media throughout the day?
- How many alerts are you getting on your computer, phone, watch, etc. that distract you and derail progress?

The list goes on and on. We all have time-wasters. As a matter of fact, our brains often need a little break to be able to refocus, but if you take too many, or if you simply aren't paying attention to them, they can take control of your schedule, leaving you feeling overwhelmed, burnt-out and dissatisfied.

Use this page to pause and reflect (maybe even journal). Here are a few questions to get you started:

- What are the activities in your day that you can identify as the biggest wasters of your time?
- When are you most interrupted in your daily work? Where are you working when you are most interrupted?
- Identify three ways in which you could limit distractions in your daily work.
- What has prevented you from implementing these solutions in the past?

Step 3 – Assess the Expectations

Next, take a critical look at the actual work on your plate.

- Is it simply more work than a full-time job?
- Have you taken on responsibilities or projects to fill gaps created due to turnover in the organization?
- Are you spending time just cleaning up or redoing work because there isn't a process or system to help you?
- Have you volunteered for too many "extra" assignments?

Now that you have the data, you are prepared to have a meaningful conversation with your manager as you think about getting to your perfect work arrangement. I'm not talking about complaining about your job; you agreed to the job and you've been doing the job. This is about using a fact-based approach to optimize your work-life balance.

> This is about using a fact-based approach to optimize your work-life balance.

The hard truth is that the speed at which we get a job done is not only based on our skill level, but also on our interest level. Things that we enjoy sometimes get more time and attention than things that are necessary because they hold our attention.

Additionally, tasks in which we are not highly skilled may take us longer than they take other people with skills in that area.

My husband, for instance, loves heads-down, focused, technical data analysis: the kind of work where you look at data in a big spreadsheet, create new ways of slicing and dicing it, and then turn it into an amazing insight that a business person can use. He can spend hours in a spreadsheet. Some nights, when there's a sporting event on TV that he wants to watch, he will stay up watching it while messing with data long after I've gone to bed. Yes, he's tired in the morning, but he was spending that time doing the type of work he enjoys.

I, on the other hand, only do the amount of data analysis necessary to get my job done. If I'm being totally honest, I start that work by seeing if I can find someone else who wants to do it for me. For me, the idea of having to stare at the screen when there isn't another face (or at least a voice) on the other side is no fun at all. I feed off the collaboration and leverage the data to drive decisions and actions. Analysis is part of my job, but not the part I enjoy the most.

This difference in our preferences means that the amount of time data analysis takes us (and what we produce as a result of our efforts) are notably different. If he and I were to switch jobs, the mental and physical time it would take each of us to do the other's tasks would be very different. A good leader will be able to quickly identify this, and, if they have the ability, will shift the work so that it matches what each member of the team likes (and is in line with their skill set), but you have to also be honest with yourself. Did that assignment take you four hours because that's how long it would take the average person, did you spend four hours on it because you were having so much fun that you lost track of time, or did it take four hours because you were struggling? The list goes on and on.

This is where being honest with yourself about any gaps in your skill set that may be impacting your workload and identifying opportunities to improve them is imperative. Most leaders appreciate when an employee is realistic about areas where an improvement in their skills could improve their efficiency. For you, it could be a major step towards finding more free time.

Use this page to pause and reflect (maybe even journal). Here are a few questions to get you started:

- Is there a tool that can help you?
- Is there a person who can coach you?
- Is there training that can improve your proficiency?
- Are you being asked to do things that drain your energy, and, as a result, you let them drag on as a form of avoidance or rebellion?
- Have you taken the role of team party-planner, the go-to for critical information, or the center of all the juicy gossip?

Step 4 – Leverage Small Changes

Once you have done what you can to optimize the way you manage your workload, you will now need to reset expectations. This won't happen overnight. It took you time to get to this point, and it will take you time to get where you ultimately want to be. If you do this too quickly, there is a possibility that it could have a negative impact on your next performance review.

Leaders are tasked with assigning a "full workload" to each person on the team. What defines "full" for each person has multiple variables, including their skills, their interests, and their overall personal speed and motivation. The closer the match between the job responsibilities and someone's skills and interests, the larger their "plate" can be. This means that what is considered "full" for one person is not necessarily the same amount of work as another person. Similarly, what is "full" for you, with a given set of tasks, may be different than what is "full" for you with different tasks.

Here are the biographies of four different people who filled the same role on my strategy team over the course of several years. They each brought unique skills to the job, and their personal style, career goals, and interests are what made them each successful. They each worked the same full-time job, but none of them did the same work.

First, there was Alex. Alex had a background in supply chain and information technology. He had previously led people and was integral in the creation of a new team, of which he was a member. He used his past experiences to create the standards, tools, templates, and processes that would be necessary for someone in his role going forward. When the time was right, Alex moved on to another role and was replaced by Claire.

Claire was a high-achiever from another department. She had joined the company a few years earlier from an outside company and was seen as an expert in her field. She had never worked in strategy, but understood the business' needs. She was able to take the tools, templates, and processes previously created and integrate them into new areas of the organization. Her background and attention to detail helped her fill in the gaps of knowledge that she had as she joined the team. Claire was not afraid to say "no" when she didn't have all of the tools she needed for the job.

When Claire left, I hired Jordan. Jordan was a highly effective individual contributor who was looking for a role that would help him get exposure to work further removed from the tactical day-to-day work at which he had been excelling. Jordan was able to take the work that Alex and Claire had disseminated throughout the company and put a new lens on it. Where Claire had taken the tools to new areas and new teams, Jordan was able to refine them for new uses. He was able to take strategies from a product level to a systems and process level.

Jordan was replaced by Drew. Drew had no experience in our industry, but was looking for a change. He had done strategy work at his previous company, but wanted to do something different. He came to the job with a fresh set of eyes and enthusiasm to learn. Drew built on the work that had been done before him by combining his knowledge from other industries to reimagine the standard tools. Using the proven framework that was already in place, Drew reimagined our reporting, ideation, and prioritization tools to give us an updated and fresh look.

The subjective nature of the definition of a full-time resource is something you can leverage as an employee, because your traits are unique to you. Unless you are in a job where your output is very specifically calculated and compared to others, your supervisor has already made assumptions about your capabilities. The good news is that you can reset those expectations slowly over a few months and work your way down to your new "full" threshold.

Do not simply work more slowly; people will notice and it won't get you to your goal. Instead, be intentional about your time:

- Slowly cut back on the extra time you spend getting a task completed.
- Start asking people when the work needs to be completed instead of rushing to get it all done as soon as possible.
- Where appropriate, begin suggesting a time by which you'll submit the work.

By changing the way that you handle work requests, you can help to reprogram the expectations the organization sets for you.

Use this page to pause and reflect (maybe even journal). Here are a few questions to get you started:

- Who is asking you to do things at the last minute?
- What can you do to slowly change the way you respond to requests?
- What messages are you sending people about how you work? Are these the messages you want to be sending? If not, what can you do to change them?

Keep Getting the Work Done

Let me be clear: I am by no means suggesting that you do less than your allotted workload. Like it or not, you already have a "contract" with your employer. If you are working an hourly job, there is likely a very clear contract in which a certain number of hours is equal to a certain amount of pay, but if you are salaried, it is more likely that they pay you a particular amount of money to get a particular job done.

What I am suggesting is that you hold your leaders and the company to the negotiated terms, which you are likely not doing today. As tedious as keeping a journal may sound, my recommendation is for you to keep the journal for at least four months. This will allow you to reset your own clock to what feels like a normal amount of work. Recondition yourself to expect to work fewer hours. Also, it may help for you to have the data in case you have moved too quickly and have put your performance review in jeopardy. It takes time to build new habits, so give yourself grace. You will have days or weeks where you slip back into your old ways, as well as times when you discover that you have overcorrected and need to adjust. Be patient.

Once you have sufficiently reset both your expectations and those of the company, it is critical that you maintain some checks along the way so that you do not get back out of control. As I've already mentioned, the company will always ask for more, but it is your job to make sure that the job is only one part of your life.

A word of caution about journaling: don't attempt to use your journal as proof that you are working. Remember, it isn't about the number of hours you show up, it is about results. This is just for your reference, in case you need to summarize what you are doing.

My friend, Casey, has been leading people for years, and she makes it known that she expects high quality work delivered as promised. She leads salaried, professional people, so she doesn't hold her team to a clock, but instead to the results. There was a time that one of her employees came to her asking for additional flexibility in terms of his job assignment. He was overloaded, stressed, and he wanted fewer responsibilities. He told Casey about all the hours he was working. Being an attentive leader, Casey hypothesized that her employee wasn't putting in the time to get the work done that he thought, so she suggested that he journal.

A funny thing happened. That employee discovered that he wasn't really working nearly as much as he thought. He was forced to admit that he was responsible for the gap, and ultimately didn't get the reprieve he was looking for. Casey admits that she never went back to him to confirm the journaling results, but she says it wasn't necessary. He stopped complaining and his job performance improved.

4

Proactively Manage Your Presence to Build Your Brand

ONCE YOU HAVE successfully secured your flexible arrangement, it is likely that you aren't going to be physically around the office as often as everyone else. That being said, be strategic with the time you are there. By doing this, you will increase your chances of being seen as a critical part of the team and reduce the push-back you might otherwise get from people who feel like they are losing access to you.

One simple way to manage your image at work is to always appear to be available and accessible. This does not mean you actually have to be available at all times, but there are some easy strategies for maintaining the appearance of availability and accessibility. These include where you meet with people, how you navigate the floorplan of the building, and the way that you manage your schedule.

These strategies play into an underlying psychology I have observed throughout my career. When people see you, you are available; when they don't, you aren't. When they can easily find time to con-nect with you, you will be perceived as available, but when they struggle to find time with you, you will be viewed as unavailable. In a traditional workplace, "available" often implies "accessible," and if you are seen as accessible, you will build your brand in a positive way.

> When people see you, you are available; when they don't, you aren't.

In "real world" terms, if you are strategic about either increasing the number of times people cross your path or the number of opportunities people have to connect with you, you will be viewed as more available and accessible. This impression is key, because this is really about managing your visibility.

Be Intentional with Your Time in the Office

If you aren't going to be in the office all day, every day, then what you do with the time you are there is even more important. You have to be strategic. The desire to build connections is part of human nature, and connections are more easily built when we see each other in person. This means that in order to get the same sense of connection you would have if you were working in a traditional, full-time office schedule, you will need to make sure that you use your time in the office wisely. I suggest you think of the time that you are in the office as if you had traveled there for work.

When I travel for work, I have an agenda. I plan ahead. I know who I need to see, what work I need to get done, and have a strategy for how to fit all of the pieces together. If you are going to be in the office less often, thinking about those times you'll be there in the same way can be very helpful. Consider creating a list of the people with whom you want to make sure you have connections. Which relationships are you maintaining and which ones are you trying to build? (Note that building a relationship takes more time and effort than simply maintaining one.)

Next, create a virtual calendar for yourself and make a schedule. Who are you going to see on this trip to the office? Who are you going to see on another visit in the future? What are the topics that are better dealt with in person? Who will you likely encounter by happenstance? Just like how you move around the building, I encourage you to make those "accidental" interactions happen—be intentional about your random interactions.

One of my employees, Bill, who worked for me for several years, was a master at this concept. Bill didn't have a desk in our building; as a matter of fact, he lived on the other side of the country. From a budget perspective, I could only afford to get him to the office every few months, so when he came, he made the most of it. When he was in the office, he had a plan, he was visible, he was in constant motion, he had something to say to everyone he interacted with, and he intentionally built connections.

Although he never worked in the same physical space as many of his coworkers, everyone knew Bill, everyone had a positive impression of him, and everyone felt a connection with him. No one even noticed how infrequently he was there. People just knew that they could count on him as a key member of the team. That's the power of being intentional with your relationships. It isn't about the amount of contact time, it's about the quality of the interactions.

Choose the Less Efficient Path

The way you navigate the floorplan of the building might be the most strategic decision you can make for your career. By this, I am literally talking about the path that you choose to walk inside your building. By being strategic about which squares of carpet you put under your feet, you can change the way people perceive you.

One of the people on my team, Katie, was a very hard worker. She would put her head down and churn out more work than anyone else. She never complained, was always available to get the work done, and would work as long as it took. Unfortunately, Katie was not appreciated outside of my department as a key member of the team; they just saw her as a cog in the wheel. Katie and I had been talking in our one-on-ones about getting her promoted. She was seen as a solid player at her current level, but to move up, we needed to work on her brand.

Katie was always at her desk; if you went there, you would find her, but that's not the point. People don't want to look *for* you, they want to *see* you. This nuance is critically important to being perceived as available, so I encouraged her to focus on being more visible for 30 days. Specifically, I asked her to change the path that she took to the bathroom and break area.

People don't want to look **for** you, they want to **see** you.

As you may have guessed, being so focused and efficient, Katie knew how to get back-and-forth to the bathroom and the break room in the most time-efficient manner. The problem with this was that her path passed very few people. For 30 days, I asked her to walk the "long" way. Instead of turning out of her desk and heading to the bathroom, I had her turn away from the bathroom and make a lap all the way around the building prior to getting to the bathroom. I asked her to do the same with the break room.

Less than a month later, when I had a meeting with my vice president about a potential promotion for her, Katie was top of mind. The little shift in walking pattern totally changed the conversation from, "What has Katie been doing?" to "Katie has been getting a lot done lately, hasn't she?"

Throughout my career, I have observed that, like it or not, we all keep a running tally of the number of interactions we have with someone throughout the day, the week, the month, or the year. The more tallies we collect on someone, the more accessible we deem that person to be. Luckily, by being strategic about how you move throughout the building, you can control the number of times someone sees you. If you sit on the second floor, try getting water on the first floor. If you sit at one end of the building, try using the bathroom on the other. If you sit in the middle of your floor, try alternating between printers on either end.

These small adjustments to your pattern will have very little impact on your overall day, but will ensure that more and more people make more and more mental tally marks for you. Besides, the more they see you, the more accessible you are. The more accessible you are, the more often you will be top of mind when an opportunity arises.

Avoid Closed Doors

Another way to increase the number of times that you are seen is to avoid the trap of going into a conference room for every meeting. Of course, there are some meetings that need to be held behind closed doors, but most meetings with three people or fewer can be conducted out in the open. As a matter of fact, for more than two years, I held almost all of my one-on-ones (including performance reviews) in an open space.

Don't panic; I'm not talking about having meetings in the cafeteria or in a break area where people hang out, I am talking about transitory areas: near the doors, in the hall, even near the coffee pot or water fountain. This works because most people do not linger in those public spaces, so any part of the conversation that is overheard is simply words without context. It's no different than sitting on a park bench while people are walking around you. No one is actually paying attention to your whole conversation, even if they do hear a little bit of it. The advantage of meeting in open spaces is that everyone who walks by you sees you.

> The advantage of meeting in open spaces is that everyone who walks by you sees you.

For almost three years, my desk was in an open workspace on the first floor of our building. That floor housed 40 people and had only two conference rooms. My coworkers fought over those conference rooms; they wanted to make sure that they were available when they needed to have a meeting. Forty people vying for two conference rooms was an arrangement that was never going to work.

While almost all of my colleagues resorted to hitting the elevator or the stairs to move to a different floor to find a conference room for each meeting, I took a different approach. Next to the employee entrance of our building, there were two restaurant booth-style tables. These lovingly became known as "Wendy's conference rooms." While everyone else was spending time running around the building, trying to find a private space, I would simply tell people to meet me "at the tables by the door." No, they couldn't be reserved ahead of time, but no one else wanted to use them, so at least one was almost always available.

Yes, being visually accessible meant that often there would be a momentary distraction; someone would walk up and interrupt us to ask a question or share some good news. I can assure you that the lost productivity associated with those occasional interruptions was greatly overshadowed by the "presence points" I received from sitting out there.

In those booths, we would have performance discussions, strategy discussions, and non-work discussions about life. Sometimes I would even meet people there just to eat breakfast or lunch with them. These tables served two purposes. First, I never had to worry about where I was going to have a meeting, and, secondly (and more importantly), every person that walked in and out of that building, or who went through the elevator lobby, saw me. I was always available.

As someone who works a flexible work schedule, I am constantly thinking about ways to make sure that I appear present in the office. This simple act meant that when opportunities became available, no one had any reservations about me being able to deliver the work. As a matter of fact, by the end of my time in that workspace, you would have been hard-pressed to find someone who would believe that I was actually working my part-time schedule (which I definitely was).

Morning + Afternoon = A Full Day's Work

This next bit of psychology is something I discovered while I was pregnant with my first child. At the time, I worked in a very long building; I sat in the middle and the bathrooms were on either end. During a regular check-up about three weeks before my son was born, my doctor noticed that my blood pressure was increasing and she wanted me to spend less time on my feet. That meant I needed to limit the time I spent in the office, because the sheer number of steps it took me throughout the day to go back-and-forth to the bathroom (something pregnant women do quite a bit) was just too much for my body to handle. Unfortunately, this was before flexible work from home was available, both from a technological and a cultural standpoint. Our policy stated that if I didn't come to work, then I needed to start using my leave days.

I didn't want to waste my leave before the baby arrived, so I talked to my manager about the situation. We agreed that I would come into the office each day, but for a reduced number of hours. Being very pregnant, sleeping in was also desirable, so I proposed that I would work the middle of each day. This is when I discovered that if people see you before lunch and after lunch, they assume that you have been there all day. They don't need to see you at seven o'clock in the morning, and they don't need to see you at five o'clock in the evening. In their mental tally, if they see you in the morning and in the afternoon when you are at

> If people see you before lunch and after lunch, they assume that you have been there all day.

work, they just assume you were there the rest of the day. They assume you were in a meeting if they didn't see you at your desk during the normal course of their activities. This is huge when it comes to managing accessibility.

Be Unpredictable

My final tip to manage your presence may surprise you. Be unpredictable. This doesn't mean you ought to be scatter-brained, unintentional, or haphazard regarding your schedule; this strategy is meant to leverage a bit of psychology in your favor. If I look at your calendar and I can see that you are always out in the morning, or always out in the afternoon, or always out on Fridays, these appear to be fixed limitations that may prevent me from connecting with you. I may come away with the impression that you are unavailable.

For example, let's imagine that you are working on a project with me and I am trying to schedule a weekly team meeting. If I want to meet every Friday morning, but that's a day on which you never work, that's a mental strike against you. If we need to be able to meet with teammates in a different part of the world who can only meet early in the morning, and you never work before ten o'clock, that's a mental strike against you. If something has come up and I need you very late in the afternoon to review something, and, as I start to look for you, I notice that every afternoon you are blocked as unavailable, that's a mental strike against you. If, however, I see a lot of time randomly blocked on your calendar, I am just going to have the impression that you are busy.

This is why being unpredictable can work in your favor. For over a decade, I worked less than 40 hours a week. I didn't do this by not working a specific day each week, or by not working mornings or afternoons: I did it by flexing in and out throughout the week. This meant that my schedule was set up such that, some mornings, I was unavailable, and other afternoons, I was unavailable, but, overall, there were very few days that I was entirely unavailable. If you were to look at my calendar across the week (or month), the time I was unavailable would look no different to you than being in an extended meeting. Your flexible work arrangement should never impact someone trying to schedule time with you any more than a regular meeting does.

One final suggestion is to ensure key teammates (and your leaders) know that if there is ever an instance where they need you, they can call. Assure them that they will never "bother" you; if it isn't a good time, you simply won't answer, but you will call them back as soon as you can.

I have lived this philosophy for years, which means that my true partners were even less impacted by my flexible work arrangement. They saw me as 100% available. I was always available when they really needed me. By ensuring your work schedule has unpredictability built into it, you can change the experience of your colleagues and better meet your own needs for flexibility.

Build Flexibility into Your Personal Life Too

For any of this to work, it is crucial that you have your personal life set up in such a way that it never gets in the way of an unexpected work request. This means that you need to organize your life as if you were working a traditional full-time job. If you have children, make sure that you have childcare available even during times that you are not scheduled to work. If you are responsible for a parent, make sure that you have full-time coverage during the entire work week even if you don't intend to use it regularly.

> Organize your life as if you were working a traditional full-time job.

Just like it's important for your work schedule to be unpredictable, it is equally important to make sure that, when work is unpredictable, you are ready to react. This may mean paying for a full week of daycare even though you don't typically use it on Fridays. That way, if something important comes up on a Friday, you are not scrambling to try to figure out what to do. It may mean that if you have a part-time nanny, you also have a back-up nanny or babysitter in case you need to adjust your schedule, or in case the regular nanny cannot come on a certain day. It may mean having a list of reliable people (such as neighbors, friends, parents, or babysitters) who you can call at the last minute when you unexpectedly have to work late.

Just like you should have back-up plans at work in case you have to be out of the office, plan ahead to have the same provisions and setup at home. There should be no reason that, given sufficient notice, you are unable to meet any work request. Remember, it's called a flexible work arrangement because it's flexible. You need to make preparations in your personal life so that you have the most flexibility possible.

When both of my children were very young, I controlled my hours by adjusting the time I left work in the afternoons. My children were in daycare five days a week, but my 32-hour work weeks meant that, most days, I was able to leave work by three o'clock. I could have arranged childcare for a shorter day in exchange for a lower rate, but, instead, I used a traditional childcare facility that was open until 6:30 pm.

Once in a while, I needed that extra time because of something happening at work. On the other days, I used that time to do things that were easier without the kids. Most of the time I used the flexibility to work out. I felt guilty about leaving the kids to go work out, but it was something I craved in order to feel centered, relaxed, and balanced. Instead of going to the gym or to a class that was on a schedule, I ran. Not only that, I ran at the daycare. Sure, I tried running elsewhere. I tried running on the treadmill in the gym at my office, as well as meeting up with friends to run together, but what worked best for me was the flexibility associated with already being parked at the daycare.

Traffic where I live can be unpredictable. By already being parked where I needed to be to pick up the children, I was able to remove that uncontrollable variable and adjust my workout time accordingly. If I got to the daycare by 3:30 pm, I could do a solid 3-4 mile run without any stress, pick the children up before 4:30 pm, and still feel like we had the whole afternoon together. If, however, I didn't get there until four o'clock, I could cut my run short so that I would still be done at the time I wanted, or I could make the choice at that moment to pick the children up later. In this way, I could optimize my workout schedule.

In the months prior to figuring out this optimized arrangement for myself, I found that I was constantly cutting my workouts short. I would look at the map on my phone, see the traffic starting to build between where I was and the child care facility, and I would start to panic. I would start to plan contingencies for missing my desired (self-imposed) pickup window. Even if I was still running, my brain was definitely not in it, and my exercise was definitely not optimized. By taking the variable of the commute out of my exercise time, I was free to make choices where I only needed to evaluate direct implications, not hypotheticals. Not only did this allow me to have a better workout, which ultimately led to better mental health for me—and probably my children as well—but it reduced my stress in the afternoon. Since stress is one of the things that makes us feel like we're not doing a good job, I started to feel better about myself.

Whether it is childcare, elder care, or some other essential non-work related commitment, the important thing to understand is that you should not establish routines or structure that will prevent you from being available during regular business hours. Success in a long-term flexible work arrangement necessitates that the company never loses. If you have established rigidity somewhere else in your life that prevents you from delivering on your flexible commitment, you will find that the company will be less inclined to continue supporting your desired flexibility.

Yes, it may seem unnecessary, given what you and your leader have agreed on, but I speak from experience when I say that business needs are unpredictable. Your best course of action is to prepare for the unknown. If you have all the pieces in place, then you will not only be able to deliver during your scheduled work time, but also when the company needs you the most. This positions you as a committed part of the team and sets you up for even greater things.

5

How to "Be There" Even When You Aren't There

WHAT IF YOU aren't going to be in the office at all? Today more than ever, people are leveraging flexible work arrangements to flourish in completely remote assignments. You might only see some of the people you work with once or twice a year, while you may never even meet others in person at all. Luckily, technology is on your side. There are lots of ways to connect with people virtually that didn't exist even a few years ago. If you want to be successful while working entirely remotely, proactively look for ways to build relationships. Some examples include thinking strategically about when and how to respond to electronic communications, leveraging video capabilities, and creating opportunities to connect with teammates on a personal level.

Strategically Respond to Email

If you can't be together in person, the quickest way to build trust is to appear available. In a totally virtual environment, this means successfully balancing different forms of electronic communication all the time. A former colleague of mine, William, shared with me that the secret to his success working remotely was that he was "intentionally responsive" to emails. He was a master at managing this inbox and it showed. No one ever waited on him for anything. He got up early to be sure he could respond to those "start of the day" emails before breakfast and then actively monitored his email throughout the day, by blocking time to do so.

If you have a coworker who lives on the other side of the world, sending them an email at the start of your day may ensure that it arrives before they go to bed, but if you have missed that window, you do yourself no favors by sending it early. You will be better served by sending that communication at the end of your day so that it will be at the top of their inbox when they log back on. Instead of focusing on that communication in the morning, you should consider connecting with people who are in a time zone closer to yours.

We all suffer from the endless bombardment of emails. In order for your information to be readily seen, it should be at the top of the recipient's inbox. If we were managing inventory at a grocery store, we would use the FIFO (first-in, first-out) method to reduce the amount of food that we had to throw out due to expiration (check out the dates on the milk at your local store if you don't believe me). However, when most people look at electronic communications, they sort it so that they see the most recent entries first (LIFO - last in, first out).

In order for your information to be readily seen, it should be at the top of the recipient's inbox.

There are lots of possible reasons this may be the case. Here are just a few:

- We have been conditioned by social media algorithms that show the most current information at the top of our feeds.
- We know that it is likely that someone else has responded to older emails and we don't want to waste time reading something "out of date" if we start at the bottom of the list.

- We have already mentally given up on the "old" ones and will use our time to try to look like we are keeping up with the ones that are more recent.
- We see the alerts for the new ones while we are working and we don't see the alerts for the block that comes in while we are offline.

Regardless of the actual science, the point remains the same. If you want to be top of mind to someone, plan your communication so that your messages show up as the most recent. To do this, you can even use technology to your advantage by writing the email when it is convenient for you and then scheduling it to be sent at a more impactful time for your recipient.

As someone who has worked on international teams for almost 20 years, I will give you my "life hack" to consider. I block a little bit of time each evening before bed to look at and thoughtfully consider responding to emails. This started years ago as a way to reduce the anxiety of the unknown and allow me to sleep better, though, today, I use it as a strategic tool to be available to teammates around the world.

Once I get my children to bed, I allow myself ten to fifteen minutes to look through my inbox to see what has come in since I logged off at the end of the day. I do this from my mobile device so that I will avoid the temptation of getting sucked in for hours. Don't think you have to do this on a mobile device. My husband has no problem doing this on his laptop; he has much more self-discipline than I. Once I see everything that has come in since the end of the day, I can decide whether there are any that I need to respond to before I go to bed, as well as which ones I should be prepared to respond to first in the morning.

I use a triage method based on the time zone of the sender. I live on the East Coast of the United States, so if there are any emails from Australia or Asia, I make sure to take care of those before bed. It is likely that they will be able to use the information they need from me while I sleep and not lose an entire day waiting. If it is from a colleague in the United States, I will likely let it sit until the morning, unless it is something quick and easy. I rarely receive emails from my European counterparts at that time of the night, as their workdays end before mine and most should be asleep by this time. However, when I do get mail from them, it goes imme-diately to the top of the list, since they will be approaching lunch by the time I wake up and will have wasted the entire morning waiting on me. I follow the same process in the morning, prioritizing Europe and Asia over the United States and Central America.

Leverage Video Capabilities

I know a lot of people hate to be on video during a meeting, but it is a fantastic way to make a human connection with someone you aren't with in person. People say they don't like video meetings because of "on–camera stress" (also referred to as "zoom fatigue"), but I really think they don't like them because the camera is an unwanted accountability partner. I love to be efficient with my time, and, every so often, I've been known to multitask. As a matter of fact, I love to do two things at once, but only when doing one doesn't impact the other. That's one problem with the camera: it prevents you from doing two things at once. What it does do is allow you to look at someone's electronic face and to let them see yours. You can see things on a human face that you can't pick up on by voice alone.

Of course, there are times when having your video on might be distracting to others in the meeting, inappropriate due to your surroundings, or could even put your safety in jeopardy (like driving). Examples might include the airport, a moving public train, a busy coffee shop, a child's sporting event, or the bathroom. Please don't *ever* call in from the bathroom with or without your video on! You should also consider company culture when it comes to eating on camera. For some teams, this is just how business is done, but for others, it may be damaging to your personal brand.

What isn't on my list is not being "camera-ready." I don't have that on the list because I cannot come up with a good reason why, as a professional person in a scheduled meeting, you would not be in a position to be on camera during expected business hours. I'm not saying that you have to style your hair or be fully decked out in makeup and fancy clothes, but are you *really* ready to do your best work if you are still in your pajamas? I've been known to go to meetings both in person and on video still sweaty from a workout, so don't let that be your excuse.

There are tons of ways to look camera-ready with very little time and effort.

- A virtual background can literally make a messy room disappear.
- A jacket or cardigan can transform a tank top into an outfit.
- A scarf or pullover can hide your most comfortable t-shirt.
- A little jewelry or a touch of makeup can make you look put-together.

Another excuse I refuse to acknowledge is when people tell me that they don't like the way they look on camera. I am willing to bet that most of us don't like the way we look on camera. It is no different than hearing yourself on an audio recording. Most of us are not camera trained and therefore don't love it. If this is your go-to excuse, let me assure you that everyone is worried about how they look on camera, and, as a result, they spend much more time looking at themselves than they spend looking at you.

Your camera being on is much more important than what is on your camera. By turning your camera on, you get to build closer relationships with your coworkers because it is easier to bond with people we see. Humans, by nature, are visual beings. By turning your camera on, you make a more lasting impression on the other attendees in your call. You are no longer a disembodied voice or a little motionless icon.

> Your camera being on is much more important than what is on your camera.

By turning your camera on, you show the other attendees that you respect their time and that you will be present and engaged. Furthermore, by turning your camera on, you have engaged with a painful accountability partner (known as other people's eyeballs) that will help you make good choices with your time.

Have a Little Fun Together

Another simple yet often overlooked way to build connections virtually is to purposely build non-work time into your meetings. We all know that the first few minutes of a meeting, whether in-person or virtually, are dead space, so use this to your advantage. There are people slowly filtering into the in-person or virtual conference room. People will be shuffling through their papers or electronic files to find the right page, the right notes, or even the right topic for the meeting. Use this time to build rapport with them.

If you were sitting in a conference room, you would likely chit-chat with the other people there, but on a teleconference or video call, people like to sit quietly and keep typing away while they wait. I promise that, when you utilize this time to connect with teammates or collaborators on the call, you will not be taking away from any actual productive

> By leveraging that time to build connections with people, you will actually be making your working time more productive.

time. Instead, by leveraging that time to build connections with people, you will actually be making your working time more productive.

Here are a few questions to get you started. I know some of them may sound like a stretch, but you'll be amazed at what you can learn if you are willing to ask:

- Ask whether anyone has something that they are excited about personally or professionally.
- Ask if anyone has any personal or professional accomplishments we can celebrate.
- If a weekend or a holiday break occurred recently, ask about what people did.
- If you are about to have a weekend or a holiday break, ask about their plans.

Unless you are very comfortable with your audience already, I suggest staying away from topics that may make individuals feel like they are not part of the group. We often think of topics like politics and religion as topics to avoid, but, depending on your group, there may be more you need to consider.

You will be amazed at what you learn about people you work with if you simply invest in these few moments at the beginning of each meeting.

Two words of caution:

- For this to work, you have to be willing to share. Don't ask a question you don't want to give an answer to yourself, and make sure that you are engaging with whoever decides to play along with you and volunteer information.

- Depending on your group, two minutes can quickly become five, and then 30 if you don't set a limit and actually keep track of time. You want to make sure this is a *part* of the meeting, not the whole thing.

Use Ice-Breakers

You can also use ice-breakers at the beginning of each meeting to set the stage for an engagement or to take a moment of mental recovery if you happen to have the opportunity to be together for longer periods of time. I try to make sure that my meetings don't go more than 60 minutes without some sort of brain break. Therefore, if your meeting will run for an hour and a half, you should have something strategically positioned along the way to give people an opportunity to mentally reset. As an added benefit, why not make it fun?

I love free online brain teasers, and there are tons available with a quick web search. All you have to do is find one that you like and go with it. Don't worry if anyone else will like it; they have no expectations. As a matter of fact, I often specifically pick ones that I do not know the answer to and leave the team hanging. You'll be amazed that, even days later, someone may finally figure it out and you'll get an unexpected email from them, which lets you know they were truly engaged in (at least a part of) your meeting.

If you need help getting started, here are a few keywords to use in your web searches:

- Brain teasers for kids. I recommend the ones targeted at children, since you don't want it to take up too much time or brainpower.
- Plexer puzzles. These are the word-based puzzles that describe a word or phrase without actually spelling it out. As an example, "cycle cycle cycle" would represent a tricycle, since there are three "cycles."
- Math puzzles for kids. These are the ones that either have a series of simple math questions and ask you to figure out a variable to solve a riddle, or give you a geometrical image and ask you to draw a conclusion about its shape.

There was a period of time when my entire team was fully remote. Not only that, but we had just been brought together under a single organization and didn't really feel like a team. We were lucky enough to have a student, Brian, working for us at that time, so we assigned him the task of finding us a weekly brain teaser.

Each Monday morning, Brian would go online, find a brain teaser (his favorite was a website that had common phrases drawn out as pictures), and send it to the group via email. At that point, the race was on. Each of us would send our guesses to him and he would let us know if we were correct. It didn't exactly start out as a race, but it quickly became one as the personalities on our team started to shine through.

At our staff meeting, he would reveal the correct answer and we would spend a few minutes laughing and joking about all the bad guesses. When the summer was over and he had to go back to school, we felt a huge void without his weekly email. As the simplicity and success of our weekly brain teaser proves, you don't have to spend a lot of time or money to build connections. What matters is that you put in the effort to create them.

6

How to Get What's Right for You

A "HYBRID WORK arrangement" is just a fancy name for a specific type of flexible work arrangement where you work from the office some of the time and somewhere else (i.e. your house) other times. Although many people and companies are currently talking about hybrid schedules as if they are brand new, the concept of working in a non-traditional arrangement has been around for decades. The difference now is that, instead of the requester being an outlier, a one-off, or a special case (and statistically speaking, likely a working mom), the stigma associated with this type of workplace accommodation has been removed due to the large number of people asking for it.

Like any other flexible work arrangement, there are a lot of reasons that someone may request this type of accommodation.

- You may have had the chance to work in a non-traditional way and dread the idea of losing that flexibility.
- You don't want to lose all that time in the car commuting.
- You don't want to be bothered by the distractions of co-workers throughout the day.
- You don't want to have to get dressed to do your individual, focused work.
- You had a change in your personal life that necessitates a change in your professional one.

Regardless of the scenario, remember that you are the one with the changing needs. The company's needs have not changed.

Today, many people have a new perspective on work-life integration, but the simple need for the company to achieve their desired results and to have employees who deliver on their commitments has not changed. Keep this in mind when you decide to talk to your supervisor about a flexible arrangement. This is about you, not about them. With a hybrid schedule, like any other flexible work arrangement, it falls to you as the employee to help the company understand how meeting your needs will not compromise theirs.

Prepare to Get the "Yes"

If you are going to pursue a hybrid work arrangement, then you will need to consider several factors in order to set yourself up for success. It's up to you and the company to decide, but if you transition your equipment to an alternate location to be fully set up to work there, your office may no longer have all the equipment and supplies you need to do effective work there.

Here are a few questions to consider before you meet with your supervisor:

- Will you have a dedicated space at the office, share a space with one or more people, or use a common space?
- Do you require double monitors, a docking station, or other specialized equipment in both locations to be successful?
- How will you ensure that any hard copy materials are always available? Will you haul them back and forth with you? Where will their primary storage location be?

There are many considerations from the company standpoint that may stand in the way of establishing a culture of hybrid work, but remember that you can only control what you can control. Equipment, space, and team norms all have to be evaluated for effectiveness in order to accommodate the new work style. I cover these in more detail in Chapter Eight. Be patient; this amount of change may take time.

It is up to you to propose the manner in which the work will get done in the new arrangement. You will also need to highlight the benefits to the company associated with your proposed schedule. It is not enough for you to want to be home in the afternoon. It is not enough for you to want to work from a remote location. It is not enough for you to want to be home on Fridays. You must be able to deliver on your commitments regardless of your work location, and it is important that you can outline that plan to your leader. Your leader should not be responsible for thinking about how this will impact the organization, it should be part of your business case proposal. (You can find examples of business proposals on my website www.makingflexwork.com.)

> Your leader should not be responsible for thinking about how this will impact the organization, it should be part of your business case proposal.

Don't fall into thinking that you are entitled to a hybrid work arrangement just because you have had a taste of non-traditional work. Just because your friend, your spouse, your co-worker, or your neighbor has a hybrid schedule, you are not inherently entitled to have one too. That is their agreement with their leader. Everyone is an individual in this scenario, so what works for one person may not work for another.

Your current (likely unwritten) employment agreement probably assumes that you will work in the office full-time, all the time. Just because that wasn't feasible for some period of time doesn't mean that you are now entitled to keep it that way. Discussions about hybrid work arrangements may be new, but flexible work arrangements are not; if you are asking for flexibility in your schedule and location, it is no different than asking for any other accommodation. Because of this, plan to treat any request for hybrid work the same way you would treat a discussion about general flexibility.

Establish Your Plan of Attack

Before you ask for a change, you should make a plan to build your presence and personal flexibility. It will be critical to your long-term success. There are more details in Chapter Four, but, as a reminder, I have summarized the two most important parts here as well.

Even before you ask for a flexible arrangement, you can begin to be more strategic with the time you are physically in the office, which will ensure you have authentic connections and are seen as a critical member of the team.

- Think through what tasks are best completed remotely and which are better to work on in the office.
- Evaluate which meetings are more effective in person and adjust your schedule to make sure you have enough time to dedicate to them in the office.
- Consider which meetings aren't impacted by your lack of physical presence in the room and try to take those from your remote location.

The key is to appear available and accessible even if you aren't around all the time. Remember, when people see you, you are available; when they don't, you aren't.

> When people see you, you are available; when they don't, you aren't.

By test-driving these strategies before you secure your arrangement, you will have a better idea of what works for you and what doesn't, and you'll be better prepared to present your business case to your leader.

Prior to getting the "yes," you can also start working on building flexibility into your personal life by creating contingency plans before you need them. It will also help you communicate how you will ensure that the company gets what it needs as a part of your business case, since you will be able to explain what type of notice you will need to get into the office. You want to make sure there are no surprises. It may mean you need 48 hours' notice, or it might mean two weeks. In either case, you and your leader should clearly outline the expectations and be ready to react when it is necessary.

Outline a Trial Period

Once you have all the pieces of your proposal in place, you are ready to have a discussion with your leader. Consider asking for a trial period, with a checkpoint to make sure that everyone is getting what they need. When your leader sees that you have built in an endpoint, you will be more likely to get a "yes" than if you approach them asking for the arrangement to be permanent. Your goal is to get a *yes*, and then prove to them that they made the right decision. Know that, like any flexible work arrangement, you may not get it right the first time. Take it a day, a week, or a month at a time and give yourself grace along the way as you redefine what works best for your situation.

Should You Move to Part-Time?

Going part-time is a big decision. It not only changes your hours, but also your compensation. Before you decide to go part-time, it's important to understand what you are currently giving to the company. Often, the difference between full-time (generally defined as a 40-hour week) and part-time (typically negotiated at 20-36 hours per week) is much more than simply 40 minus the agreed-upon number of hours because most full time roles simply aren't *just* 40 hours.

Before you decide to embark on this specific type of flexible arrangement for yourself, you should be aware of the possible tradeoffs and research your company's policies to learn more. Some examples of the tradeoffs include:

- A reduction in pay (which may have natural break points at 20, 30, or 32 hours)
- A reduction in benefits, or the portion of your benefits that the company contributes
- A reduction in vacation time (often prorated based on the number of hours you work)
- A reduction in bonus payouts or other auxiliary compensation

By following the EVAL steps from Chapter Three, you will know if you really need to make the financial tradeoff. Since you are about to walk away from money and benefits, I feel like a quick review of those steps is in order.

Every Hour Counts

Create a log of all your working hours for a week. This is a snapshot of your current reality. The key is to not be "strategic" in picking a week to monitor. Don't pick a "good week." Start now, start tomorrow, start the next time you log on. Create a virtual time clock for yourself and, over the next five business days (or seven if you're known to work on the weekend), record every time you start and stop working.

At the end of the week, add up the total number of hours that you worked during the week, the total span of work on the clock (meaning the earliest start time and the latest end time each day), and compare each of those numbers to a 40 hour work week. The gap between the number of working hours and 40 is what you will need to overcome to get to a reasonable full-time schedule. The blocks of time between the beginning and end of your workday is the normal cadence of time with which you have to accomplish those 40 hours. This data is critically important because the company is currently used to you producing a certain amount of work within certain time periods. Capturing this data will ensure that you don't change too much too fast.

Value Optimized Work

Slowly begin to adjust your schedule. This can happen in one of three ways.

1.   Shorten your overall workday.

The workday is defined as the time you first start working until the last time you stop working for the day. This may make you feel happier because you will have more time before the start and after the end of your workday. The goal of this approach is to produce the same amount of work, even if it means taking fewer breaks throughout the day to compress your schedule.

For instance, if you normally log on at 6:30 am before the house gets busy and are still dabbling at work after dinner, your body may feel like you have worked a thirteen-hour day even if you only actually worked for eight or nine of those hours. If this is the case, try not logging on until 8 am, or making sure you log off before dinner.

You will need to be more focused on work during those hours in the middle, but you may instantly feel better about your schedule.

2.   Work fewer hours throughout the workday.

This is different in that, instead of squeezing your working time closer together, you actually reduce the total number of hours you are working. To accomplish this, you will want to identify ways to optimize your schedule or be more efficient with your tasks.

You may be able to find times when you are working at a reduced level of productivity. If this is the case, you can use that "down time" to take care of your personal to-do list. Examples are taking a break to work out, running errands when the stores and roads are less crowded, or spending time with friends and family.

If you can make the mental shift to stop working when it isn't necessary, you may find the balance you need already exists in your schedule.

3.   Mix and match the first and second approach to customize
     for your needs.

In this approach, slightly adjust either your beginning or end
time while also making an effort to be more efficient in what
you do throughout the day. This could mean that, on
Mondays, you work a longer day so that you can work a
shorter one on Tuesday, when you have a lot of personal
things to do. It could mean that you meet a friend to work
out on Wednesdays at lunch because you found a big block
of non-productive time in your work schedule. It might mean
that you stay up late on Thursday to get ahead for a weekly
Friday meeting, but once that meeting is over, you can call it
a weekend unless there is an emergency.

There is no right or wrong with any of these options, just
know that the only way to find more balance is to do one
of them. You cannot
work the same number
of hours in the same
span of time and feel

Same schedule, same feelings!

any differently about your schedule than you feel today. Same
schedule, same feelings!

Assess the Expectations

Once you know what is currently on your plate and have a grasp of how and when you are working, the next step is to take a candid look at what you are doing.

- Is your day filled with tasks that are of value to the company, or have you picked up additional work along the way that you can shed?

If you find that you are doing work that isn't highly valued, look for ways to politely step away. Don't think of this as not fulfilling your commitments or as letting the group down. Instead, consider that this may be the perfect opportunity to give someone else a development opportunity.

- Have you overcommitted to extracurricular activities at work because you like them?

Is it possible that the things that bring you the most joy take a disproportionate amount of time in your schedule and you have never noticed? Maybe you haven't noticed because you like the activities and the way you feel when you do them. Maybe you are doing it to counterbalance the real work that you don't find as engaging as your extracurriculars. Either way, if you need more free time to find balance, cutting back on the "extras" at work might be the right thing for the moment. The good thing about those volunteer positions is that they will very likely still be there when you are ready to jump back in.

- Are you doing work that isn't assigned to you in order to pick up the slack for someone else?

If you find that this is the case, it can be tough to correct, because, at the end of the day, the work has to get done. Here is where you have to step up and advocate for yourself with your leader. Get your facts together and make sure your supervisor knows what is happening—but tread lightly. You don't know what conversations the leaders have when you aren't around, so you don't want to sound like you are being judgmental or like you consider yourself to be better than anyone else. You don't know everything that is going on in your co-workers' personal and professional lives, and it is a serious mistake to make assumptions about them.

- Does it take you longer than your peers to perform certain tasks?

If you don't know how to answer this question, take a moment and talk to your peers. If you find out that this is the case, it is likely that there is a tool that can help you, some training you can take, or someone who can coach you on how to be more efficient. Don't be too proud to ask for help. After all, this is about you getting what you need to be successful.

These are just a few examples of places where you can cut back without impacting your performance or pay, but it isn't an all-inclusive list. Be honest with yourself about what you are doing during the day, and whether you (and the company) are getting out of it what you need. If the answer is no, then find a way to stop doing it.

Leverage Small Changes

I am a self-proclaimed science nerd and love the saying, "How do you boil a frog? Very slowly." It is sort of like the phrase, "How do you eat an elephant? One bite at a time." Though I can't imagine why I would ever want to eat an elephant (or boil a frog, for that matter), since a frog is cold blooded, it is hypothesized that you could boil it alive without it jumping out of the pot by simply heating the water up slowly enough. That is exactly what you are going to do to achieve your desired work-life balance.

You are going to make many small adjustments to your schedule, moving at a pace slow enough that no one notices. The farther from your ideal state your current state is, the longer it will take to get there. Be patient. It took you a long time to get to this level of work and overall schedule, so getting back in balance will not happen overnight.

If you have done all this and you still feel unbalanced, then you should think about going part-time. That's where I was. Most of my friends could handle working full-time, but I needed more flexibility than I could have in that type of traditional arrangement, so I started my journey part-time—and I've never looked back.

7

What about Leaders Who Want Their Own Flexibility?

I WISH I could tell you that I know the difference between leading teams while working full-time in the office and leading them while on a non-traditional schedule, but I've only done it part-time, so I can only provide that perspective for you. Fortunately, just about every other leader you will meet has done it traditionally, so I am confident that you can find someone else to provide you with that perspective. As a matter of fact, you may be living it right now.

What I do know about leading people while working part-time is that it's no different than doing any other part of your job while working part-time; you must be intentional. In this case, though, the specific thing to be intentional about is your relationship with your team. The higher you rise in an organization, the easier it can be for you to become disconnected from the people and to get consumed by the business, the strategy, the numbers, and the results. At the end of the day, your people are the most important part of your job. I believe that if a people-leader is not excelling at developing their people, then they are not excelling at their job.

> If a people-leader is not excelling at developing their people, then they are not excelling at their job.

Build Authentic Relationships

If you aren't in the same physical space with your team all the time, then using the time to connect when you are together in person is critical. If they have a hybrid or remote work arrangement, the little bit of time that you get face-to-face is even more valuable.

When I get to choose, my preferred method of meeting with people individually is over food. I believe strongly in the psychology of sharing a meal to strengthen relationships. I'll go for lunch, coffee, breakfast, or even dinner with my team when I have the opportunity. I believe that taking the time to sit together over food shows them that I value them not only as a part of the team, but as a part of my life. Also, since I am being intentional with my time away from home, and I have to eat anyway, I might as well use that mealtime as part of my workday.

One of my fundamental tenets of leadership is that you should meet your teammates individually, where they are, and that you should flex your style to meet theirs, not the other way around. To that end, one-on-one connection should be driven by the needs of the employee, not you. For example, here are some types of one-on-ones I organized with four people who worked for me:

- Tami and I were both working moms who value effi-ciency and like to eat. We bonded over food, so we would go out to a long lunch once a month and solve all the world's problems while we ate.
- Cindy was a remote teammate who thrived on structure. We would meet for 30 minutes each week and follow a pre-written agenda where she would present and I would ask questions.
- John was a manufacturing guy. He liked routine and, for most of his career, he had worked for leaders who liked formal meetings. Consequently, so did he. John liked

to sit in a conference room for exactly one hour each month and go through everything he needed from me, so that's what we did.

- William was a remote teammate who was a senior level individual contributor. He didn't need me for the technical part of his job, but appreciated feedback on strategy and approach. We had a meeting on the calendar once a month, but more often than not, he would text me that he needed something and I would call him on my drive home that afternoon. By the time we got to the scheduled meeting, we were both already up to date.

The method and location didn't matter. What mattered was that I was building authentic relationships with them by being willing to do what was most comfortable for them. The point was not to make me comfortable, the point was to focus on the employee and what made them comfortable. One-on-one time should be *their* time. Yes, I need status updates, but by letting my employees drive the agenda, the setting, and the cadence, they knew that they were important. When you make people feel safe, important, and connected, your work schedule isn't an issue.

Put Your Team First

As a leader, my team always knows that they come first. They have my cell phone number and I encourage them to use it. They can text me. They can call me. They can email me. They can send me an instant message. They can schedule a meeting. They have full access to me, and they know I will make time for them.

One of my strategies for maintaining a flexible schedule as a leader of people is to block 30-60 minutes on my calendar at the end of each workday as "no meetings." That doesn't mean that I am not available to work, but if I can avoid getting pulled into a meeting and can finish the day sooner, I will take advantage of that time. I don't have to say anything to anyone, because the blocked time on my calendar simply looks like any other meeting.

The real secret of the "no meetings" time, however, is that my leader and my team know that it is really held for them. They don't need to ask if they can talk to me during that time, they can just freely schedule over it. By blocking this time on my calendar, I have guaranteed that I have time available every day specifically for them. The general public, however, does not get the same freedom. In this way, I ensure that the people most important to me are never negatively impacted by my part-time schedule.

Of course, there are times when people need me during the "no meetings" time, but they will almost always send me a note to ask if it is okay to schedule over my time (just like they would if they were scheduling over any other appointment on my calendar). The beauty of this is that it gives me the opportunity to make a decision. Do I want to have that meeting at the time they proposed, or do I want to suggest an alternative? The control shifts from the meeting scheduler to me and grants me the freedom to manage my own schedule.

Be Prepared to Work Anywhere

I probably shouldn't admit it, but I work a lot from what is jokingly referred to as my "mobile office." By that, I mean my car.

I find that the times when I sit alone in my car provide excellent opportunities to catch up with people. I don't use it for meetings where I need to take notes and be totally focused, but my commute time is a perfect opportunity for a quick connection.

I use it to say:

"Hi, I was just thinking about you and wanted to check in."

"I heard something that made me think of you. Do you have time to chat?"

"I know that there is something big going on in your life and I wanted to see how you are doing."

Throughout the workday, I may not have time to have those types of conversations while at my desk, but the time while I am in transit is the perfect opportunity.

I also have a hotspot that I use to connect my computer to the internet from any parking lot, and a setup in my car so I can work effectively while parked. For me, this is critical to maintaining my balance. After all, the reason I went part-time was so I could be more available as a mother, and, as the mother of two growing children, I spend a lot of time in my car waiting for them. Whether I am waiting in the carpool line or outside a practice facility, I make sure that I can be productive while I wait.

In this way I can make my schedule even more unpredictable, appear available at times when people may not think I am, and focus on work without the potential distractions associated with working in the office. The ability to work remotely, specifically in my car, has been instrumental to my ability to continue to move up the leadership ladder. This doesn't mean that I give the company more hours than we previously agreed-upon, it simply means that I have a greater ability to flex those hours throughout the week.

I know I'm not working too much because I didn't stop tracking my time after I established my part-time arrangement. More than a decade later, I still do. I just do it differently now. Instead of writing my hours down to pace myself so that I don't go over my agreement too early in the week, I proactively look at the week ahead on my calendar and plan out when I am going to work and when I am not. I look for times where I know I am going to be able to work from my mobile office, and I add them up. I look for those meetings that happen at strange hours of the morning or night, and add them up. I look for times that I have things I want to do for myself and my family, and I block them off. Once I account for those things, then I know my starting point, and I fill in the rest of my 32 hours accordingly.

Sure, as a leader, I may be asked to work extra hours here and there, but it is all about an overall balance. If, for instance, the company gets 35 hours this week, then, next week, maybe they only get 30. At the end of the next two-week period, they've gotten 65 of our agreed-upon 64 hours. They won an extra hour over the course of 2 weeks, but I didn't lose—I got some extra time back in the second week.

Perhaps the most important lesson you can learn regarding how to lead while working part-time is that you should widen your lens and look at time on a more macro scale. Instead of thinking about the hours per day, or even per week, think about the hours on the whole. Depending on your job, maybe your timescale is two weeks, a month, or even a quarter. However, if you look broadly enough, you should be able to find balance, and, more importantly, stay within the agreed-upon boundaries. This assumes that, as a leader, you are a salaried (exempt) worker. If this isn't the case, then you will have to maintain your scale at the appropriate level for the hours that you are tracking.

Make Your Flexible Schedule Visible

The last thing that I have done as a part-time leader is something that many people dread. I made my part-time work very visible. This may seem counterintuitive to my previous advice to not make a big deal about your personal needs, but there is a turning point along the leadership journey where you no longer have the luxury of blending in. Instead, you have the obligation to help change workplace culture for everyone else.

Just a few months after I started my first director-level role, I shared with a senior leader that, all of a sudden, I worried about what I wore to work, that I felt the pressure to be "put together" in a way that I had not previously felt. I just felt like there were eyes on me all the time. Her response was simple. "Of course people are watching you. As one of the few women at your level, you are setting an example."

> But there is a turning point along the leadership journey where you no longer have the luxury of blending in. Instead, you have the obligation to help change workplace culture for everyone else.

The organization that I was in didn't have a history of many female leaders, and, at the moment, I was "The One." Over the next three years that I was in that role, the team would evolve to a point where there was a small cohort of female leaders. At the beginning, though, I was new to the team, and the team was new to having a female leader, especially a young(er) one. By the time I had been in my role for six months, I think I had been invited to a one-on-one by over half of the women in the organization to talk about career development. I would share my strategies for work-life balance and talked more than a few of them out of switching to a part-time schedule. Each one of them followed my EVALuation method, even though it didn't have a name yet, and were able to get what they needed without giving up money or their benefits.

During this time, I realized I had to face my fear of rejection, the awkward looks, the talks behind my back; I had to accept that people would be watching me. As a leader, if you haven't experienced this feeling yet, just know that your moment is coming and be prepared. It is at that moment, where all of the time you have spent juggling, preparing, and compensating in the background is replaced by doing it in front of everyone. It is at that point in your career that you have the obligation to bring all the messiness that comes along with being you (in my case a working engineering mother) out into the open. It's terrifying, but I speak from experience when I say that the reward is well worth the risk.

I've never been one to hide the fact that I have a personal life away from work. Everyone around me knows that I have children. I talk about my children at work and I share information about what's going on in my personal life. That's my personal preference. Lots of my colleagues do not have any desire to be an open book, but, at some point, you are the leader to whom others like you look to as a role model, someone who can provide them with advice and guidance. More importantly, you are the one that your fellow leaders look to understand the "new norm," what is acceptable, and what they can expect from those who come after you. If you are not brave enough to put yourself out there, how can you expect the people you lead to be truly authentic with you?

One particular moment of "real life" came one afternoon when I needed to call in to a monthly financial review with our senior leadership team. The meeting was scheduled for 2:00 - 3:30 pm, a totally normal hour in the day for a meeting, but, for me, that was carpool pick-up time. For those readers who may not know how carpool works, a school might let students out at 2:15 pm, but you have to be in line for carpool by 2:00 pm in hopes of picking up your children by 2:30 pm. (No, it doesn't make any sense; it's just the way it works. Maybe I'll tackle that in my next book.)

Since I couldn't be at my desk for the beginning of the meeting, I did what I needed to do to make it all work: I took the call from my mobile office. I made sure I was parked in the carpool line by 1:58 pm, opened my laptop, turned on my mobile hotspot, and logged into the meeting. As people started joining in on the video call, everyone could see that I was sitting in the driver's seat of my car. One of my leaders asked where I was, and when I said that I was in the carpool line, all the other leaders chimed in, asking if it was "safe" for me to be on a video call. Clearly, they had never sat in a carpool line, so I explained the process, reassuring them that I was safe. At approximately 2:20 pm, the cars in front of me started to move, so I turned off my video (incoming and outgoing) and proceeded to listen to the call as I slowly rolled forward through the line.

Before three o'clock, the children and I were home, I had my computer back on my desk, and I made a very subtle re-entry onto video (which no one even noticed, due to the screen sharing during the meeting). By the time the meeting ended at 3:30 pm, there I was, on camera, sitting at my desk like normal. The meeting was uneventful, but I'm pretty sure several of my co-workers had discussions with their spouses about carpooling that very night!

Model Success in the Messiness

Like many others, the pandemic gave my coworkers a literal look inside my home life. While some people worked hard to make theirs invisible, I used it as an opportunity to show parenthood and work as a blend. I chose very early on in the transition to work-from-home to keep my camera on most of the time in order to make it easier for others to do the same.

I shared my workspace with my children as they attended virtual school while I worked. In the background of my meetings, people could see second grade virtual learning, they could see fifth grade virtual learning, they could see brain breaks and wiggle breaks and virtual P.E. They could see me turn around and answer questions. They also saw that, sometimes, my children would break down and need a hug or just want to sit in my lap. What they saw was that I could still work while taking care of my family's needs.

I realize that not everyone would feel comfortable doing this, but I did this from a place of safety. I have a 20-year track record that shows that I can be successful at work. If you have the ability, I encourage you to model how you are able to be successful in the messiness so that others around you can be empowered to do so as well.

8

What about Leaders Who Want to Embrace Flexibility?

AS A PEOPLE-LEADER myself, I've learned quite a few things. When it comes to leading people, you have a choice. You can either force your team to conform to your needs, or you can adjust your needs to accommodate each individual. As with most things, there is no right or wrong way to lead teams, but if you, as the leader, are willing to customize your approach to meet each teammate where they are, people will flock to you. The ability to make everyone feel like they are heard, valued, and important to the overall mission can position you as the leader everyone wants to work for.

I am a big believer in the concept of servant leadership. This concept, accredited to Robert K. Greenleaf, asserts the primary role of a leader is to support their team. However, that's not what I am talking about. What I am talking about is being willing to have conversations about what people want from their job and how the company is doing at meeting their needs.

Now more than ever, it is likely that one or more of your employees will be asking you for flexibility. Maybe you make the decision to provide flexibility to aid an employee who has child or elder care needs. Maybe you will provide flexibility out of the desire to support physical and mental health. Maybe you will make the decision to leverage flexibility as the most important retention tool in your managerial toolbox. As long as you can ensure that the work is getting done, I challenge you to be flexible.

Embrace the Idea That Work Can Happen Anywhere

If you are serious about flexible work, you are going to have to let go of some of your "old school" leadership strategies, specifically "leading with your eyeballs." When everyone is together physically, it is easy to see work happen, but it is also easy to mistake presence for productivity. When your team isn't within eyesight, you have to trust that you have assigned the right amount of work, as well as accept that when high quality work is delivered, it doesn't matter when and where it happened.

You've made it this far, so I want to say thank you, but equally importantly, I want to address a contradiction that you may have noticed. I provided tools to manage your presence in Chapter Four, but just warned leaders against mistaking presence for productivity. The scary truth is that both are true. As an individual, it is critical that you get your work done (a measure of your productivity), but you also benefit from intentionally managing your presence (to support your brand). As a leader, however, you need to be aware that if someone is really good at managing their presence, you could be lulled into a state of complacency if you aren't actively keeping up with their work output. Sorry, but that's the truth! Being a good leader takes a lot of effort.

Once you embrace the mindsetthat you don't have to physically see the work being done to ensure that it is actually being done, you can remove some of the constraints you put on your current team. If you don't make it a requirement that your employees must be able to come to your desk on a regular basis, you will no longer be limited to job candidates living in your immediate area. Additionally, as traditional work constructs continue to be broken down and altered, top talent will no longer be limited to jobs in their geography and will be able to choose not only what role they take, but who they want to work for.

> Top talent will no longer be limited to jobs in their geography and will be able to choose not only what role they take, but who they want to work for.

For you, this means that being the best leader around is no longer going to be good enough. You are going to need to be a truly excellent leader, or at least someone working towards excellence (which is all anyone really wants from their leader). You are going to have to up your game when it comes to traditional leadership skills and also practice harder skills like trust, communication, and performance management.

The reality is that, with today's technology, work can happen anywhere. Whether it is a teleconference by the pool, a video call from a parking lot, or a group huddled in person in a conference room, work is work. Just like fixing something around the house, if you have the right tools and the willingness to try, there are lots of ways to succeed.

As much as we know this about ourselves, it's hard for many leaders to give up their control, which is necessary to provide flexibility. Unless your team is strictly paid by the hour, you are paying them to get a job done, so that's what you need to let them do, even if they don't do it the way everyone else does.

I have seen work happen on a dining room table in the middle of a game of cards on a moonlit porch as the rest of the household slept, as well as under a tent at the beach as fish were being pulled in from the surf. These places became offices because of the work that was happening, not because they had traditional setups with a desk, monitor, and chair.

In each instance, the company was getting exactly what it needed in order to be successful in the moment, and the teammate was getting exactly what they needed in order to feel balanced and energized. Understanding that there are countless different ways of delivering a work product is what sets excellent leaders apart from the average ones. More importantly, as companies shift to using hybrid workforces, teammates are going to be looking for leaders who have embraced this sort of creativity.

Leverage Your Listening Skills

Being a leader who supports flexibility in their organization is no different than being a good leader in general. Listening, seeking to understand, and being there for the team are all anyone really wants from their supervisor.

In order to be there for your team, you must first build authentic relationships with your employees. A great leader knows more about the individual than whether or not they met their performance objectives over the last quarter. They know what they like about their job, what they hate about their job, why they come to work every day, what motivates them, and what brings them down. No, you don't have to be everyone's best friend, but if you want people to feel like they can come to you when they need flexibility, they need to know that they can open up to you about other aspects of their life. Often, the desire to have a flexible work arrangement is tied to a personal need. If your team doesn't feel like you have any interest in them as people, then

> A great leader knows more about the individual than whether or not they met their performance objectives over the last quarter.

why would they come to you for help solving their personal problems?

Seeking to understand someone else's perspective can be tricky, especially for the employees with whom you relate the most. If you are truly trying to understand them, then you have to avoid the temptation to impose your personal framework onto their lives. The closer your life experience is to theirs, the harder this may be. For instance, if you have a structure in place that supports you in terms of child care or parent care, you may assume that everyone else in a similar type of situation could benefit from using that structure when this simply may not be the case.

At the same time that I was having my son, there were two other women in my department who were also pregnant with their first child, and, coincidentally, each with a son. To an outsider, we all looked the same. We were all technical women in our late 20s/early 30s who worked in the research and development department, but we all had our own approaches to handling the necessary work travel after the boys were born.

I had the luxury of being able to take the baby with me on trips since my parents had retired. I worked out a plan that would allow me to go outside of the company travel policy and book directly with the airline, making it possible for me to book my travel as "infant in arms" and to use my airline points to secure a seat for my mom.

Kate and Angela, on the other hand, didn't choose to take an entourage everywhere they went. Kate leveraged FedEx's overnight capabilities to make sure that her milk didn't go to waste. Throughout the week, she would pump milk (often in an office or bathroom at the international manufacturing facilities she traveled to) and store it in a hotel refrigerator. The company agreed to pay for her shipping expenses as a part of her overall travel budget.

Like Kate, Angela leveraged overnight shipping at the end of the week. However, she found that getting dry ice was just one more thing she didn't have time for, so she devised a plan that involved using freezer bags of water packing inside a cooler bag. She would ask the hotel staff to keep the whole package in their commercial freezer until the delivery driver arrived. Where Kate had expenses associated with a cooler box, dry ice, and shipping, Angela only needed the company to cover the cost of the shipping.

The point of this anecdote is not how each of us managed to survive that first year. Rather, it's to show that, if our leader had treated all of us the same, then at least one of us wouldn't have gotten the support we needed. Lucky for us, we didn't have a problem asking for what we needed—and our department was willing to provide it.

Similar to not assuming that one solution will work for everyone, also avoid jumping to the conclusion that everyone else is struggling with the same things you did. Let your employees tell you what they need and then attempt to understand how you can help them. This means that if you are in a different phase of life than your teammates, you have to understand the ways in which the world has changed since you were in their shoes and how that may be presenting them with unique challenges. This is also true if you are a younger leader, as your older employees may have difficulties in their lives that you have not yet experienced.

When I first started working, I was assigned a desk, a desktop computer with a wired mouse and keyboard, and a landline phone number that went directly to the phone that sat on my desk. If you needed to reach me, you had two options: you could call me or email me. In either instance, I had to be at my desk to answer. All my office work was done at that desk and most of my files were saved to the hard drive on that desktop computer. It wasn't until later in my career that I was issued a laptop and remote access to be able to work from home (where I was still tethered to a wall by the ethernet cable). If that first workstation set-up was the baseline by which I judged an entry-level employee's ability to do their work in today's environment, it would look much different than the current reality.

Today, most of my files are saved in the cloud so I can work on them from any device, from almost anywhere in the world. In my household, there are four people who share three laptop computers and two tablets. If someone is on one of the devices, I simply grab a different one and open my files. As a matter of fact, most of this book was written in my mobile office using my phone. If I can do this today, I can only imagine the different ways a book could be written in the future as technology advances.

Look for Ways to Make Technology Work for You

If you had told me 20 years ago that I was going to write a book, I would not have believed you. As a chemical engineer, that was not a logical step on the career path pitched to me by my faculty advisor. If you went a step further and told me that I would write it almost exclusively using the voice-to-text feature on a mobile phone from my car, I would've thought you were from another planet. When I started working, phones were exclusively used for talking, and, if you were a budget-conscious young engineer like me, even the talking was saved for nights and weekends, when the rates dropped.

Thankfully, we now have a variety of options for getting work done effectively. As a leader, you have to remember that, as fast as things have changed in the last twenty years, that change will only accelerate in the future. This is why listening is so important. When you open your mind, allow yourself to hear your employees' struggles, and encourage them to bring creative solutions to you, you can discover possibilities about which you would otherwise be unaware.

Do they have a device, a gadget, an application, a set-up, or anything else that you were unaware of that will not only make them more effective, but that you can share as a best practice with other people on your team? Are you willing to let them try something to see if it could improve everyone's efficiency and effectiveness? In order to be a supportive leader in the new age of hybrid work,

> It is imperative that you see all options as possibilities and attempt to envision a way to make them work as opposed to identifying reasons why they won't.

it is imperative that you see all options as possibilities and attempt to envision a way to make them work as opposed to identifying reasons why they won't.

- If someone suggests that they can work from the beach for a month (which I have done successfully), look for ways to make that work. Of course, you should ask questions to be sure that all the scenario planning has been done. Examples might include:

   "What will happen if you need to come in?"
   "How much notice will you need?"
   "Who will cover any last-minute requests?"

Start with an open mind. Don't jump to telling them "no" because you can't imagine being able to do it yourself. Instead, take the mental journey with them as they explore the possibility.

- If someone proposes that they can work a split schedule that entails mornings spent working from home, the middle of the day from the office, and the afternoon back at home so they can be there for the school bus (which I have done successfully), be open to giving it a try for a week. Before just saying "yes," however, make sure everyone understands what will happen if something

important is required at a time when they are not scheduled to be in the office. Ask how they plan to handle the
transit time in the middle of the workday from a scheduling standpoint. Also make sure they consider what will
happen on days when there is no school at all. The point
is to start from a "yes" and then make sure plans are in
place to ensure your team will still be able to deliver the
necessary results even when confronted with occasional
obstacles arising from this unique work arrangement.

- If someone proposes working some days from home and
others from the office (I haven't done this personally, but
have watched personal connections make this arrangement work successfully), assess the merits of the plan
and then ask how they will pick their days. Make sure that
they have a plan that explains what work they intend to
do at each location. Ask them what it will look like if the
schedule needs to change. Assume they have a thorough
plan, but ask probing questions to verify.

You can find these and other examples of questions to consider on my website www.makingflexwork.com.

If you give your team the creative license to design a work
plan that works best for them individually, they will feel supported. You may even be able to get better, more consistent,

higher quality work from your team because they will want to do it for you. By being willing to have the conversation, even if you aren't able to give them everything they want, they will know they are part of a team that is valued.

> You may even be able to get better, more consistent, higher quality work from your team because they will want to do it for you.

Set Clear Expectations

As the leader, it is important that you set clear expectations for employee performance. It is even more critical to have these expectations clearly outlined if you are going to provide flexibility in the delivery of those expectations. I suggest you go back to the fundamentals of objective setting as outlined by Doran, Miller, and Cunningham in 1981 and make them SMART.

- Specific: What do you want the person to deliver?
- Measurable: How will you know if the product they deliver is good?
- Achievable: Is this something they are capable of doing within the agreed-upon arrangement?

- Relevant: What does the business need and how can those needs be met?
- Time-bound: When would you like this task or project to be done? Is there any benefit to them being done sooner? How do they fit in the overall priority?

Most importantly, these expectations need to be in writing. When you lack the ability to drop in to chat with someone to clarify your intentions at any moment, you have to make sure to get it right the first time. I believe this is why many leaders are scared of flexibility. They lose the right to change their mind on a whim.

Establish Routine Check-Ins

As with everything in life, change is inevitable, so be prepared for it. You should establish a process for evaluating how the flexible arrangement is going for both the company and the employee, and determine the frequency of these discussions. You should also align on how you will react to changes in performance, changes in business needs, and changes in organizational structure. If you don't already have predetermined time with your employees for this type of discussion, it is important to establish it as a part of the flexible arrangement. If that time already exists, simply add it to your agenda.

At these check-ins, it's important to know how you will determine whether everything is on track. Here are some examples to consider:

- Will it simply be based on the delivery of a work product?
- Is there anything subjective that could impact the continuation of the arrangement?
- What sort of time would each side need in order to change the agreement?

You don't have to write it all down (you can if it makes sense for you), but you should think it through like any other business contract. Everyone needs to understand they will only be in this arrangement as long as it is working for everyone.

Communicate Your Non-Negotiables

As you think through the role each person plays on your team, there will be areas where you will feel more or less comfortable being flexible. It is important that you communicate this early and often with teammates so they can prepare and respond accordingly.

- Proactively think through the options that are and are
  not available to each person based on their role and the
  business' expectations.

It's important to be open and honest with teammates whose
jobs allow for less flexibility. For instance, if they need to
be hands-on in a laboratory in order to deliver on their job
responsibilities, or if they have in-person customer service
responsibilities, their options are more limited than someone
who does independent data analysis at their computer all day.

- Identify the times/occasions when you need everyone
  to be together in person and which allow for virtual
  connections.

Do you need the team to be together physically on the first
day of every month in order to deliver the business results?
Do you need them to meet in person twice a year for strategic planning meetings? Do you want to bring them together
for a specific training or team-building purpose?

I encourage you to let the team know what you need as soon
as you know you need it, so they can prepare and adjust their
arrangements so that they will be available. I specifically
challenge you to think at least two weeks ahead. If you can
tell your team that you would like everyone together in two

weeks, your team should have built the support system to be set up for success navigating that change.

For example, realizing at the close of business that you need everyone together the following morning does not give your team enough time to react. You, and they, will end up frustrated—and with the perception that flexibility isn't a viable option.

Just like being clear with your expectations, another reason that other leaders shy away from allowing flexibility is that it requires them to know and proactively communicate what they expect from their team, and when they need it. If you decide to embrace flexibility, it is no longer acceptable for you to procrastinate or change your mind at the last minute. You have to be proactive enough to provide the time and space for your team to deliver on your needs.

With a little proactive thoughtfulness and planning, your team will flourish. Trust me, I've been there and done that... and even written a book about it.

Don't Think Flexibility Is Only for Working Parents

The key to supporting working parents is to not focus on the fact that they are parents. Approach their issues the same way you would when helping any other employee. Having parental responsibilities should not make a difference when it comes to adjusting one's schedule. When we focus on parents (specifically mothers), we can quickly lose sight of the fact that everyone, at any stage in their life, has unique needs.

The toughest stage that I had to navigate over the course of my career was the period of my life when I was single and lived alone with my dog. Sure, you can board a dog when you travel, but trying to figure out how to drop off and pick up my pet when I was a one-woman show was exponentially more difficult for me than sorting out similar logistics with my husband regarding our two small children at home. Later in life, I hit another rough patch when my dad died and I started getting the occasional call to help my mom. Luckily, she is super independent, but there are still times that, as a

> Everyone, at any stage in their life, has unique needs.

single woman, she needs to be driven to an appointment or dropped off somewhere.

Being a manager-mom is the only way I've ever experienced being a manager. As a result of this, I've mentored both men and women throughout the organization, served as an example of what it's like to move up in your career as a parent, and developed unconventional ways to support working mothers.

Having a toddler and a newborn as I entered into management meant that I had to establish boundaries for myself, my team, and my leaders quickly. I also had no choice but to model what a working mom looked like to my team, starting from the earliest days of returning from maternity leave. Sometimes, that meant delegating more to my team than other managers. Other times, it meant taking an in-person meeting via phone from the mother's room. I was never shy to let my colleagues know the importance of feeding my newborn, and I was amazed by how supportive the men were to my needs as a mother. Because I put it in front of them, they felt comfortable sharing stories about their wives, daughters, and sisters, and the struggles that they had encountered along the way. These conversations eventually led to a greater understanding within the organization of what we could do to support working mothers (and fathers).

The women in the organization also quickly realized that I could serve as an ally for them, as well as an information source when it came to understanding policies, procedures, and practices related to parenting while working. When I had my children, I knew exactly what I needed for my family situation, but this was not necessarily the case for the women who worked around me. What is good for one mother is not necessarily ideal for another. For some women, more time off with their families was the perfect solution to their problems, but for other women, being able to ease back in over a longer period of time was desired. Some women wanted to totally disconnect while on leave, while others wanted the ability to know what was going on and not get too far behind. Slowing down to listen to each woman and finding out what was most important to her allowed me to help them tailor their leave to fit their needs within the company's policy.

Take the example of Christi, who was job hunting at the same time that she was trying to grow her family. The company policy did not ensure maternity leave for people who had worked for less than twelve months, which meant if she got pregnant within the first three months of her employment, or if she didn't carry her baby full term, she wouldn't have the financial protection the other mothers had. If I wanted her on my team, I would have to get creative, so

I leveraged the policies, adding a signing bonus equivalent to the six weeks of short-term disability leave that Christi would potentially miss out on if she was to deliver during her first year. Sure enough, Christi found out that she was pregnant about a month into her new role. As her due date approached, a young woman from Human Resources had the tough job of telling us that Christi wouldn't get the standard leave benefits. Instead of panicking, we just smiled, knowing it was already taken care of.

But it isn't always the moms-to-be who need help obtaining leave to take care of their children. As a leader, I have also helped dads navigate the journey into parenthood. Andy and his wife wanted to limit the amount of time their new baby was in daycare for the first six months of the child's life, but there wasn't a paternity leave policy in place. Creativity was needed again. By using a flexible schedule, he was able to take off every Friday for a few months to stay home and bond with the new baby while also supplementing the support they received from extended family and formal childcare.

As a leader, I have also helped employees navigate getting their job done while caring for aging parents. Nicole was an Atlanta-based team member with an aging mother who lived in New York. Nicole had the "on the ground" support of her brother for most of her mother's day to day needs, but when she began to have serious health issues, Nicole needed to be there in person.

At first, she and I didn't know exactly what she needed in terms of flexibility, but we knew that a flexible work arrangement of some kind was needed, and that the specific type might evolve over time. Over the course of a few months, she traveled when she needed to and simply worked remotely while she was there. That worked for a while, but then what was required of her in terms of parental care had grown to such an extent that she couldn't effectively manage it and her work obligations at the same time. At that point, we prioritized her work so she could triage it during any downtime that she had, reduced her overall workload, developed a plan for last-minute meeting coverage, and, eventually, we reduced her time so she could really focus on her mother.

You may find that when you open up to your team, they will tear down their walls and be more open with you. This is a good thing, but be prepared for questions about and interest in your own experience as a result. A lot of people have never had a leader who values them as a whole person, so they may open up in unexpected ways. For me, this has come in the form of questions... lots of questions. Newlyweds (both men and women) and married fathers have asked me about what it was like to have two children and to work. Single women have asked about what it was like to be married, to have two children, and to work. Senior leaders have asked about what it was like to be married to an engineer, to have children, and to work. The list literally goes on and on.

Remember, the only way to understand and change workplace culture is to talk about it. As a leader (specifically a parent-leader), you have to set the stage and be willing to put yourself out there. That advice that I got years ago to always keep in mind that people are watching holds true. Once you start to put more of yourself out there, more and more people will start to take notice. When you have their trust and attention, you can influence the future—not only that of the company's workplace culture, but even that of your teammates.

> The only way to understand and change workplace culture is to talk about it.

What about Hybrid Work?

If you are serious about supporting hybrid work, there is more work for you than just saying *yes*. Unlike part-time or remote work, hybrid work arrangements have the ability to impact everyone. When you begin to give some people (or everyone) the ability to flex in and out of the office, it can affect the way your space is utilized, the technology needed for the job, and even how people interact (including the potential for jealousy). As the leader, there is a lot to consider, but if you have the time and energy to do it right, you can position yourself as the person, department, or company that everyone will want to work for.

This is by no means an all-inclusive list, but here are a few ideas to get your creativity flowing:

Space Considerations

Traditional office spaces were not designed for hybrid work. Most are either filled with doors and large private spaces that will be underutilized in a hybrid environment, or have open floor plans originally intended to increase collaboration, but which have very little privacy as a result. Neither of these configurations is inherently bad, but neither is optimal for hybrid organizations.

- If you plan to have people using video at their desks, how will you minimize the visual distraction of the rest of the office environment and the associated background noise?

- If you plan to have video calls only in conference rooms, do you have enough of them to support your team?
- What if more than one person is on video calls, from their desks? How will you control the background noise? Who will provide the headsets?

Equipment

Many people have specific workstation requirements to be effective at their job. Some of these may be legitimate needs, while many others are just very strong preferences (like having multiple monitors). Either way, thinking about how you will make sure that everyone can work successfully in a hybrid environment isn't something you can turn a blind eye to in the hope no issues will arise.

- Standard corporate conference rooms are not generally set up for a hybrid meeting, so AV upgrades may be needed.
- What specialized equipment will need to be duplicated for hybrid employees? Who will pay for it and how will its use be controlled and monitored?

- Will people have assigned seats in the office or will there be a sharing strategy? If there won't be assigned workspaces, what is the plan for sharing them? Who will share? Where will supplies be stored? How will you ensure there is a space for everyone when they need it?

Team Norms

Generally speaking, if there is another human in your space, you look at them when you talk. This means that the virtual teammate can very quickly be cut out of a discussion (even in a conference call with video capability) unless everyone is focused on not letting that happen. This can even happen if the majority is virtual. The few in the room will have a full conversation and literally forget the others are present unless they are intentional in their inclusion of their remotely located teammates.

- What topics will be discussed in a totally virtual environment, which require a face-to-face meeting, and which can be conducted in a hybrid environment?
- What types of meetings will require video? Which will be audio-only for the remote team members? Are there meetings where, even if two or more people "can" be

physically together, the entire meeting will be held virtually to level the playing field?

- How do you make sure the remote teammate is included
  in "offline" discussions and decisions? What happens
  with information that is shared in the hall, the time
  before/after the meeting, or the occasional drop-by
  discussion?

Conclusion

It's Your Game, You Define Success

There is no universal definition of success, just a desire to make all of the pieces fit together. Each of us has a unique puzzle. Yours may have 5000 pieces, or maybe you only have 100. Maybe your puzzle is a giant floor puzzle, or maybe it's travel-sized. Maybe your pieces are big, or maybe they are small. It is up to you to understand your puzzle and to decide on the best way to put the pieces together.

I remember trying to teach my son how to put a puzzle together when he was very young and how frustrating it was for both of us as I showed him the way I was taught to do it. First, you are supposed to identify all the straight edges and put the rest of the pieces back in the box. Next, you build the frame. Then, you finally get to fill in the middle part of the puzzle.

My son refused to follow this method. To him, the idea of sifting through the box in order to find a straight edge piece was simply unreasonable when he could easily identify all of the pieces necessary to build the main character located somewhere in the middle of the puzzle. Why, then, was he not allowed to simply build the character first, and then another and another? After building several individual pictures, he could connect the giant chunks of completed puzzle and then finish by attaching the straight edges, since they generally have nothing to do with the image on the puzzle.

In life, as with puzzles, it is easy to compare the way that we do things with the way others do them, and to make assessments about which strategies are good and bad. The reality is, however, unless someone lives in your house with your family and your pets, with your obligations, your preferences, and your skills, they should neither be expected nor obligated to make the same decisions as you. Your choices shouldn't be judged based on the way they make their decisions, either. We are all different.

Understanding that work is only one part of your life may be the most important takeaway you get from this entire book. If you are a team leader, understanding that work is only one piece of each of your employees' lives is also critically important. Yes, you are paid to do a job, to make money for the company, and to be successful in your work life, but without taking the rest of the pieces of your life into consideration, the work itself is meaningless.

At the start of my flexible work arrangement, my team leader and the team knew about it, but most other people did not. When I was presented with the responsibility to proactively look for opportunities to change what people knew about me as a way to change the culture, I cautiously embraced the challenge. Just like I did, I encourage you to look for ways to make flexibility visible to the broader organization so that everyone can see that there are more possible roads to success.

Whether you choose to make any changes based on the steps that I have outlined, or whether you decide to make other changes in your life, my hope is that you come away from this book with a new perspective. Maybe you are working too many hours, maybe you are trying to do too many tasks that aren't yours, maybe you are being inefficient with your work time, or maybe you just need time to sit and breathe and rethink your current situation. All of those are important outcomes.

You are responsible for defining success, and, luckily, you are also responsible for making the decisions that will lead to that success. What an amazing amount of control! Don't be afraid to try something new and be bold enough to advocate for yourself.

Review Inquiry

Hey, it's Wendy here.

I hope you've enjoyed my book, and that you've found it both useful and fun. I have a favor to ask you.

Would you consider giving it a rating wherever you bought the book? Online book stores are more likely to promote a book when they feel good about its content, and reader reviews are a great barometer for a book's quality.

Please go to the website of wherever you bought the book, search for my name and the book title, and leave a review. If able, perhaps consider adding a picture of you holding the book. That increases the likelihood your review will be accepted!

Many thanks in advance,

Wendy Cocke

Will You Share the Love?

Get this book for a friend, associate, or family member!

If you have found this book valuable and know others who would find it useful, consider buying them a copy as a gift. Special bulk discounts are available if you would like your whole team or organization to benefit from reading this. Just contact wendy.anderson.cocke@gmail.com or go to www.makingflexwork.com.

Would You Like Wendy Cocke to Speak to Your Organization?

Book Wendy Now!

Wendy accepts a limited number of speaking/coaching/training engagements each year. To learn how you can bring her message to your organization, call or email wendy.anderson.cocke@gmail.com or visit www.makingflexwork.com.

About the Author

Wendy Cocke is the Founder of Engineering Leadership Solutions LLC where she provides management coaching and leadership development.

Wendy is a chemical engineer by training and spent over 20 years leading technical teams in Fortune 500 companies. During that time, she led large, international projects and coordinated resources across time zones, borders, and languages. After moving into leadership roles, she managed teams spanning R&D, Manufacturing, and Supply Chain, focused on increasing sales, improving quality, enhancing design, and reducing costs. She has been integral to the launch of two major medical devices and provided support during numerous supply chain interruptions to reduce customer impact.

About ten years into her career, when her oldest child was still an infant, Wendy pursued a flexible work arrangement that would allow her to balance all aspects of her life. She was told that, though the company supported her desire to pull back, her career would stall and she would never move up in the organization. Little did they know that the change to her work schedule would be the catalyst that would propel her career.

Wendy lives in metro Atlanta with her extended family (lovingly referred to as the rolling circus), which includes her husband, two kids, mother, and grandmother.

Wendy can be reached at: wendy.anderson.cocke@gmail.com or www.makingflexwork.com.